Faces and Places Along the Railway

Faces and Places Along the Railway

Elizabeth A. Willmot

GAGE PUBLISHING LIMITED
Toronto, Vancouver, Calgary, Montreal

Design by Mario Carvajal

Canadian Cataloguing in Publication Data

Willmot, Elizabeth A., 1918–
    Faces and places along the railway

ISBN 0-7715-9472-0

1. Railroads—Ontario—History. 2. Railroads—
Ontario—Stations. I. Title.

TF27.06W54   385′.09713   C79-094264-X

1 2 3 4   BP   82 81 80 79

Printed and bound in Canada

Contents

Acknowledgements

I wish it were possible to individually thank all the people who so generously shared their personal memories of Ontario pioneer railway life with me. The list is long, and many of these people have become my dearest friends. I extend my appreciation to Grace Mills of CN Public Relations for her constant encouragement and kindness, and to Edna Staebler, author of *Food That Really Schmecks*, who said, "Of course you can do it!"

In a very special category is Mrs. Cela Sloman of Clinton, Ontario. She and her husband, the late Fred Sloman, graduated over 1,000 children during their thirty-nine years of teaching in Ontario's first railway-school-car. During that time they also brought hope, sunshine and adult education to lonely trappers, railway-section men and woodsmen in isolated areas of northern Ontario.

Symbolizing the hardy breed of railwaymen of the "Steam Era" is the loveable 82-year-old Herbert Stitt, retired CPR engineer, who considered every facet of his work to be worthy of pride and respect. He has an endless repertoire of stories filled with humour and warmth, of railway life along the branch lines. To countless other railwaymen I owe sincere thanks, especially to Fred Worthington and his crew, who ran the way-freight train out of Orangeville with me as a passenger in the caboose. This experience was the ideal way to explore the historic line of the Toronto, Grey and Bruce Railway (now CPR).

Librarians, town clerks and small-town newspapermen all gave me valuable information. I would be remiss if I failed to mention the courtesy of Helen McNeil and her staff at the George Locke Library, Toronto; Lynda Moon, history librarian at the Northern District Library, Toronto; Helen Delaney of the Midland Library; Mrs. Lloyd Pipe who compiled the Tweedsmuir Book in Londesborough; Mr. Omer Lavallée, Corporate Archivist for CPR Montreal; Miss Dorothea Druce of Kingston; Lenore and David Thomas of Parry Sound; and Mr. John Marsh, editor and publisher of the Amherstburg *Echo* newspaper who brought to life the railway story of his town.

On the last run of CNR's #6218, I met Mr. Leonard Appleyard of King, Ontario, who has photographed almost every railway station in Ontario, as well as in every other Canadian province. Mr. and Mrs. Appleyard have taken me along on many wonderful "station hunts," and mapped out other routes for me along which I discovered many abandoned, historic, railway stations.

For many years I have had the good fortune to be a friend of Mr. Andrew Merrilees, an authority on international railway history with a particular interest in the early Ontario railway companies. He graciously corrected factual errors which otherwise would have appeared in this book.

I am also very grateful to the Explorations Program of the Canada Council for its generous support, which enabled me to write *Faces and Places Along the Railway*.

To my understanding husband, Bill Kettlewell, my eternal thanks for his patience, guidance, and confidence.

Picture credits

Photographs appearing in "The Schoolhouse on Wheels" story, from the Sloman collection. Reprinted by permission.

Winter of 1947 photographs appearing in "Nostalgia Fills the Branch Lines" story from the collection of Herbert Stitt. Reprinted by permission.

Photograph of the Brockville tunnel, page 67, from the archives of the Toronto Star. Reprinted by permission.

Photograph of Londesborough Station, page 28, courtesy of Mrs. Winona Pipe of Londesborough. Reprinted by permission.

Strip map of Picton, page 41, by Bill Kettlewell.

To

the pioneer men who built and ran
the many small railways in Ontario,
and to the people who thrilled to
the sound of the steam whistle

Introduction

"Here comes the train!" Those first, magic words were uttered on September 25, 1825.

It all began in England when the first public railway for steam locomotives was opened by the successful run of the engine, "Locomotion," on the Stockton Darlington railway, with its inventor, George Stephenson, at the throttle.

"Here comes the train!" was the cry of the thousands of spectators who came to watch, or scoff. And it was quite a sight: a string of elegant coaches, usually horse-drawn, was being pulled by a four-wheeled steam locomotive, and the engineer on board was wearing a tall, beaver hat.

Buoyed by the enthusiasm and obvious enjoyment of his audience, Stephenson warned his firemen to "Keep her hot, lad," then opened the throttle wide. The train responded with an unheard-of speed—fifteen miles per hour.

In Canada, a similar performance won the hearts and stirred the imagination of spectators crowding the streets of Toronto on May 16, 1853, to see James Good's locomotive, "The Toronto." It initiated passenger service on the Ontario, Simcoe and Huron Union Railway. At every hamlet and crossroad between Toronto and Aurora, that exciting cry could be heard above the clanking and whistling of the tiny wood-burner locomotive: "Here comes the train!"

Every nation has filled its archives with statistics about its railways, but the stories that made the railways unique never found their way into vaulted archives; they remained in the memories of the men who were "The Railway."

Even though mankind has learned to travel through space at incredible speeds, we are still thrilled at the sight of a train. The engineer at the throttle of the locomotive has always been a hero, and who can resist waving to him as he highballs down the track?

Down the line, every face and every place has its treasury of railway lore. So much of it can never be recorded—it's too late—but the search must never stop.

Places Along
the Railway

TILLSONBURG

When you asked friends in Tillsonburg to meet you at the station a few years ago, you had to be very specific. Even though the population was less than 10,000, thirteen passenger trains used to stop in town every day at no less than four different stations. But times have changed in Tillsonburg, and as in so many other southern Ontario towns, only freight trains now use the lines. Passenger service is finished—at least for the present. Two of Tillsonburg's stations are positively handsome, and it's depressing to see their waiting rooms unused and their platforms empty.

Probing into the history of Tillsonburg's railways whets even the appetite of those with only a half-hearted interest in railways. The names of the lines themselves tell a story. There was the Brantford, Norfolk and Port Burwell Railway built in 1878, which started off in Harrisburg and never got beyond the centre of Tillsonburg, a distance of just 34 miles. Then there was the Canada Southern Railway, also built in the early

Tillsonburg Michigan Central Railway Station

1870s, running in a straight line (for the sake of economy) between Fort Erie and Amherstburg. It later became known as the Michigan Central, then the New York Central, the Penn Central, and presently is simply called "Conrail."

In direct competition with the Canada Southern, another railway was built at the same time by the Great Western and was called the Air Line. It ran parallel to the Canada Southern and went from Fort Erie to Glencoe (near Chatham) where it joined Great Western's main line and continued south to Windsor. This line is still in existence, but it, too, has changed names since its original charter. It was amalgamated with the Grand Trunk in 1882, and since 1923 has been part of the Canadian National System.

There was a branch from the Air Line which cut off the main line at the Tillsonburg Junction station, ran into the heart of town and continued into Brantford and Harrisburg. This was built under the charter of the Brantford, Norfolk and Port Burwell Railway but was always operated by the Great Western. The railway station built in Tillsonburg for this line surely must have been one of the most attractive ever built by the Great Western Railway. Artists and photographers are constantly seen with their easels and tripods, trying to capture its Gothic charm.

The railway in Tillsonburg with the most ambitious-sounding name was the Tillsonburg, Lake Erie and Pacific Railway. It began in Port Burwell and limped into Tillsonburg, 16 miles in all, and just 3,000 miles short of its goal. No railway company ever had more financial distress. All its building materials were castoffs from other companies, and its rolling stock consisted of one secondhand boxcar and a decrepit locomotive. ("Poor But Proud" would have been an appropriate motto for this company.) Despite its bank debts and disgruntled investors, it set about developing Port Burwell as a port of entry for American coal. This development sparked the Canadian Pacific's interest, and they decided to lease the ailing Tillsonburg, Lake Erie and Pacific Railway in 1904—no doubt, much to the relief of the cynical investors of the almost bankrupt lively. In the fall of 1824 George Tillson, an employee of the Van Norman Company in Long Point which manufactured cauldrons and stoves, was exploring the Otter Creek, rumoured to be rich in ore deposits. He camped overnight at the head of the Otter Creek (the present site of Tillsonburg) and decided it would be an ideal spot to found his own town. Later that year, in partnership with his nephew Harry Tillson and Mr. Ben Van Norman, he bought three lots. The first of many industries George Tillson was to develop began when they built a forge on one of the three.

Wild animals and Indians still roamed the country when George Tillson brought his family to settle in the area in 1831. When the community was surveyed and laid out in 1836 it was called Tilsonburg—somehow, the second "l" in the name had been omitted. This error remained until 1902 when an Act of the Ontario Legislature changed the name of the town to the "Town of Tillsonburg," with its rightful two "ls." Tillsonburg was incorporated as a town in 1872, and its first mayor was Edwin D. Tillson, son of the town's founder.

George Tillson was a man with decided ideas on town planning and when Broadway Avenue, the main street, was being laid out he was criticized for the width he allocated to it. It is 100 feet wide, which is a record for main streets in Ontario. He is quoted as having said, "Broadway is as wide as a pair of oxen needed to make a complete turn about without having to back up before going ahead." Right up until the early part of this century, horse racing was common along the Broadway, and during the winter months children on toboggans and sleighs sped down the full length of the street, manoeuvering between pedestrians and horse-drawn vans.

There seemed to be almost an obsession in Tillsonburg over streets and their names. One street, for instance, changes its name four times within a half-mile. It starts out as Baldwin, then becomes Oxford Street, and after crossing the Otter Creek it changes once again to Simcoe Street, and then eventually becomes King's Highway #3.

Because of the little "empire" George Tillson established

Tillsonburg "Airline" Station at junction

T.L.E. & P.Ry. The line between Port Burwell and Tillsonburg was officially opened on January 4, 1896, but the maiden trip of the first passenger train took place on the last day of 1895 — and what a trip that was. The single coach was loaded with passengers, and while the train was still within shouting distance of Port Burwell, the locomotive slid off the tracks and sank into deep mud. After the company was transferred to CPR in 1904 the line was continued to Ingersoll, and in 1908 it was extended to St. Marys. It was a busy line back then and remains so today.

In Tillsonburg, colourful history was not confined just to its railways. The entire story of the town's development is

Tillsonburg CPR Station

...tility between rival railways never actually occurred ...e great boom in railroad construction in the 1870s. ...were certainly some moments requiring the ultimate ...acy.

...le the Great Western Railway was creating a short cut ...or, by building a "Loop Line" from Fort Erie to Glen-...re it up with the company's main Windsor line), ...ailway company was racing in an almost parallel line ...outhern Ontario, from and to the U.S. border, trying ...re of the American business. This was the Canada ... Railway (later leased to the Michigan Central Rail-...l it ran from Fort Erie via St. Thomas to Amherstburg. ...m the sod-turning ceremony of each railway, competi-...een the two was deep-felt and stimulated, perhaps, by ...papers who kept their readers well-informed of the ...f each company.

...873 the Canada Southern came to Amherstburg—or, ...ct, it came in to Gordon, almost two miles from the ...ut the Canada Southern itself received a setback. ...make Chicago its western terminus did not continue ...for the railway. As usual, there was the problem of a ...f funds, and when the line ran into a frog pond in ...progress came to a halt for all time.

...mplete story of Amherstburg's railroading days is ...the chronicle of this part of southern Ontario. ...were the first white people to claim possession of ...their post was called Detroit. It was taken by the ...3, but twenty years later the post was given back ...rstburg took on new importance, and in 1804 ...nt of the town of Amherstburg began. ...old fort has been almost completely restored ...Fort Malden. Guided tours reveal the impor-...played during the War of 1812, and in the ...er and Lower Canada in 1837-38. The very ...n famous meeting between Shawnee

leader, Tecumseh, and Major General Isaac Brock, commander of the British Forces, took place on August 13, 1812, can still be seen on the grounds of the museum. Fort Malden was taken by the American Army in 1813, and after the Treaty of Ghent, was restored to the British on July 1, 1815. When walking through the quiet streets of Amherstburg today, admiring the inspiring churches and buildings of the 1800s and the many elegant old homes, it is difficult to realize that strife existed there for so many years.

Mr. John Marsh of Amherstburg, historian, keen railway enthusiast, publisher and editor of the Amherstburg *Echo News*, has kept files of all the railway news since the entry of the Canadian Southern Railway. He quotes from a diary entry of the late C. W. Thomas of Amherstburg, dated 1872, in which Mr. Thomas records the arrival of the first train: "The first train over the C.S.R. from St. Thomas arrived in Amherstburg today." And the newspaper noted that the railway company obviously was not superstitious, because the train came in on Friday, November 13, 1872. A celebration took place but its description was not noted.

The Canada Southern was leased by the Michigan Central Railroad on January 1, 1883, and in 1884 the main line was diverted from Essex to Windsor, a distance of just under 17 miles, reducing the original Essex to Amherstburg section to the status of an unimportant branch. Fortunately the stations in Amherstburg and Essex are still standing, and the latter is presently being restored. It is a stately fieldstone building which gives the impression that each stone was chosen for its individual beauty. Its port-cochère with its high, arched entrances must have been a beautiful sight for passengers arriving at the station in horse-drawn rigs.

According to John Marsh's *Echo* reports of the railway, irregularities were frequent along the branch line running between Amherstburg and Essex. Long-time residents of both towns never tire of repeating tales about the "Plug," their affectionate title for this train which faithfully shuttled back and forth. In an article dated August 18, 1933, the station was

in Tillsonburg with his various mills, he was regarded with considerable respect by the town's residents. It was rumoured that when he died he would return in the form of a turtle, to cast an eye on the management of his town. Oddly enough, not long after Tillson died in 1864, an enormous turtle was discovered roaming the valley of the Otter Creek. It was captured and put on display in town, where it was regarded with mixed curiosity.

Long-time residents of Tillsonburg have almost forgotten the sounds of bells and whistles, which at one time seemed to govern their lives. Beginning at 7 A.M. the town-hall bell would ring. This was the signal for every factory whistle in town to start blowing, summoning labourers to the job. Then at 12 o'clock, noon bells and whistles blew again for lunchtime, and an hour later they announced its end. Finally at 6 P.M. they proclaimed the end of the working day. When you realize that every passenger train blew its whistle on approaching and leaving, as well as at every crossing, it becomes apparent how few minutes of silence there were in the town.

For Mr. Bill Popham, shoe-store owner and life-long resident of Tillsonburg, the railway was an accepted and very necessary ingredient of everyday life. His home was just two doors away from the Great Western station on Hale Street, and he is sure he spent most of his early days watching trains at that station. Always, the highlight of the summer was the excursion train that took entire families to the church picnic at Port Burwell. A train of at least 10 coaches was needed to carry the crowds. Mr. Popham said that he and the other children never wasted a moment by sitting down on the train. Instead, they raced from coach to coach, eating ice cream cones which cost just two cents each. He thinks he made a record one time when he ate twenty cones before the train pulled into Port Burwell! Other trains which regularly stirred up a flurry in Tillsonburg were the Niagara Falls Specials, the ever-popular circus trains, and the annual arrival of the Orangemen on July 12th. Their parade formed up on the station platform, then headed down Broadway.

"Hoot" Fleming's horse-drawn jitney bus, which met every

train and transported passengers to hotels in town, was another popular attraction at the station. Orville "Hoot" Fleming is gone now, but his son, Ted, still remembers riding on his father's knee on the jitney bus, waiting for the arrival of passenger trains. Orville's loud hooting of his horn upon his arrival at each hotel earned him his nickname. "Hoot" drove a wooden coach owned by Barret's Livery that was pulled by two horses. It would carry about eight passengers with their luggage stowed on top. A sleigh-bus replaced it in the winter, and in 1924, a motorized Model T Ford Bus was introduced. Travelling salesmen who came to Tillsonburg were always popular with young Ted Fleming because they could be counted on to hand him at least a five-cent piece, and frequently they would also offer a drink of cold orangeade at the Arlinton Hotel.

John "Never Sweat" Cowan was another familiar figure at Tillsonburg stations around 1914, accompanied by his horse-drawn mail waggon. John was never known to hurry, and summer and winter he wore the same, heavy, winter coat buttoned up to his neck. The boys in town took delight in playing pranks on old John, and their favourite was to unhitch the traces from the whippletree so that when John called "Giddap" to his horse, it trotted off leaving John and the waggon sitting at the station — a sight which never failed to elicit great guffaws from the boys.

Jitney busses, mail waggons, circus trains and celebrating Orangemen aren't seen around the Tillsonburg railway stations now, but in a quieter way, each station is still active. Possibly the last event causing any excitement around the railway stations though, was a jim-dandy derailment in 1916 down near the old Junction Station. A freight car burst open when it toppled over, spewing out crates upon crates of butter and a well-known brand of toothpaste. Before railway police had an opportunity to reach the disaster scene, the wreckage had been mysteriously cleaned up and removed. Equally mysterious was the local pool hall's remarkable bargains in slightly bent tubes of toothpaste, just five cents each, and in pounds of butter at a mere ten cents.

< *Tillsonburg Great Western Station (now CNR)*

Each of Tillsonburg's stations is different in style, ranging from simplicity to true period elegance. It's sad to think that the oldest and most historic station may be slated to go. It's the Tillsonburg North station, built by the Great Western Railway in 1879. The long, narrow windows and doors all have the Gothic arch, and the years have mellowed the red brick, bringing the warmth of age to its colour. The doors were painted green at one time, and they too have improved with age; they now resemble the illusive shade found in a old piece of Chinese jade. No matter where one stands to view this lovely old station, the effect is superb. But when you stand on the arched bridge on Tillsonburg's famous, wide Broadway Street, which spans the old Great Western Railway tracks, you especially realize what a pity it would be if progress removed this handsome, historic building and bridge.

R...
tio...
prog...

to be e...
the c...
the area...
Plans to...
smoothly...
shortage o...
Michigan, ...
The c...
contained i...
The Frenc...
the area, an...
British in 170...
to the Unite...
River at Amh...
the developme...
shortly...
Today the...
and is known a...
tant role the fo...
rebellions of Up...
stone upon whic...

referred to as "a social centre where folks went to have a chat with friends." The writer claimed that the Plug was monarch of the travelling world, carrying the inbound and outbound freight, human and otherwise, to and from the 'Burg.

"The shabby little M.C.R.R. station was a sort of social centre, and it was a customary pastime for some folks to saunter down to the depot daily at train time just to see who was getting on or off, and have a friendly chat. The Echo reporter need only go to the station to get copy for the society column. . . . Who was visiting the Who's, and Who of the Who's were galivanting elsewhere. Train time to many folks along the railroad lines was the big event in their more or less uneventful lives, and a trip on the train, a real adventure. The smoky appearance of the old Plug creaking, grating, hissing, blowing and ringing afforded a thrill to the youngsters not even exceeded by the drone of the Zeppelins in this day of wonders."

When the Plug completed its chores for the day, it was bedded down for the night at the roundhouse, where night watchman Michael Meehan kept a loving eye on his charge. When the Plug was prepared to the complete satisfaction of the crew for its morning trip, its highly-polished brass and nickel gleamed so brightly, it made the viewer squint.

Another article, clipped from the Amherstburg Echo News, recalls the disaster involving the Plug that occurred on August 10, 1907. A carload of dynamite being shunted into Essex blew up, killing two members of the train crew, and "nearly obliterating the town of Essex. This explosion cost M.C.R.R. $25,000. Property damage in Essex ran into the hundreds of thousands of dollars." The reporter concluded in this manner: "The old Plug has certainly made history in its day."

When you walk along Sandwich Street in Amherstburg and approach the corner of Richmond Street, always a busy scene of railway activity, you find the abandoned right-of-way of the old Canada Southern Railway.

Amherstburg's station was opened in 1891, and continued to serve the town until 1969. The Fort Malden Guild of Arts and Crafts was aware of the historic value of the railway sta-

Amherstburg waiting room window

tion, and how appropriate it would be for their association. Through the generosity of Mrs. J.R. Gibson, the station was donated to the Guild. Visitors to the old station now see classes being conducted in pottery, weaving, painting, drawing, and children's arts and crafts. Members of the Fort Malden Guild of Arts and Crafts gave their time and talents to the cleaning and restoration of the station, and have called the building in honour of their benefactor, the Gibson Gallery.

Fortunately, the lovely, old, red-brick station stands in its original spot, still in mint condition and still a place that draws crowds from the town. It's an interesting place to visit and many artifacts remain to remind you of the days of the old Plug. In midmorning and again in late afternoon, there is an unexpected bonus for visitors who come on sunny days: the leaded, plate-glass fanlights of the east and west windows act like full-colour sun dials, casting rainbow patterns on the floor and walls. Young and old still make special visits to watch this delightful phenomenon.

THE SCHOOLHOUSE ON WHEELS

If you would like to see the largest schoolyard any teacher ever had to watch over, pick up a map of northern Ontario and follow the CNR line running between Capreol and Foleyet — 148 miles! This is where Fred Sloman taught school for thirty-nine years, in a converted CNR railway coach. Through the courtesy of CN, his school car would be dropped off on a siding and four days later moved to the next siding, where another group of children was waiting for an introduction to education. Sufficient homework was left behind with each child to keep him busy until the school car returned, after completing its month-long circuit. Along this line you will see names such as Stackpool, Laforest, Ostrom and Ruel, and in-between these tiny communities lived the children of railwaymen, Indians, trappers and lumbermen. These were the pupils of this unique school.

The plan for this wilderness school system took place in Fred Sloman's imagination during World War I when he was recuperating from injuries. It seemed a great pity to him that so many of the fine boys who were his comrades in hospital were totally uneducated. He resolved at that time to search for a way to ensure an education for children living in remote areas. Back in Canada, his first teaching post was in a small village which hadn't had a school teacher for over two years. And he discovered that there were children in even more out-of-the-way areas who had never seen a school, and who probably never would. He was determined to reach them and asked for permission to travel on foot along railway lines, carrying the bare essentials for teaching. Fortunately however, Mr. J. B. MacDougall, assistant chief inspector of Ontario schools — who was equally concerned with the problem — suggested having a railway coach converted into a moveable schoolhouse, complete with living quarters for a teacher and his family. Nothing could have appealed to Fred Sloman more. The Canadian National Railways donated a wooden coach, and on September 19, 1926, Canada's first school on wheels sat on a lonely siding near Nandair, waiting for the arrival of its first pupils.

Inside the coach were Fred Sloman, his wife, Cela, and

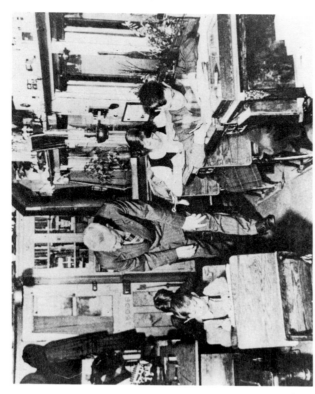

Fred Sloman teaching in CN school car

their two-year-old daughter, Joan. It was not a foreign atmosphere for the family. Fred's father had been baggage-master in the Grand Trunk station in Clinton and had built his home according to railway-station design, including the familiar telegraph operator's bay window. It was just a stone's throw from the station, and the sounds of passing trains and steam whistles were familiar to the family.

Although the lettering on the side of the old wooden coach read "School on Wheels," the simple word "Welome" would have been equally appropriate. Their desire to provide an education for children of the north country was only a portion of Fred and Cela Sloman's plan. To dispel loneliness was also their aim, and the warning given to them to keep doors locked and window blinds drawn at night was completely ignored. Burning kerosene lamps in the coach windows, and pots of flowering geraniums, daffodils and narcissus blooming on every window ledge served as an invitation to wives of railway section men, trappers, and men who "rode the rods" across Canada during the depression years. No one was ever turned away, and no man was ever regarded as a tramp. Cela Sloman mended clothes for these men, fed them and packed a lunch for later use.

Constant surprises during their years in the school car are still discussed in the Sloman home today. Children were so eager to learn, nothing would keep them away from classes when the car was in their area. Most children had great distances to come through bush land, travelling by canoe, dog team, or on snowshoes. Two brothers, just six and eight, pitched a flimsy tent where they lived summer and winter, cooking their own meals. At Stackpool, where the only sign of habitation was an abandoned trapper's shack, 134 pupils had come out over the years and graduated. So keen was their desire for education, Mr. Sloman had to accelerate the courses to keep up with their progress. After just a month of schooling, most children were able to compose and write simple letters.

An Indian family of six children, mother, father and grandmother, arrived at the school one morning and the father announced that he had brought along his children for their education. Throughout the day, the entire family listened in silence, and when the closing of books by the other pupils indicated the end of the school day, the Indians stood up and the father said, "Now my children have been educated." They disappeared into the bush and were never seen again.

The cost of running the school car was $5,500 a year, which included the teacher's salary, school supplies and fuel. Even in the 1920s, the wages must have been barely adequate, but Fred Sloman was not concerned with accumulating more money than was needed at the moment. If his bank account reached $100, he would take as many boys as he could to Toronto, where civic officials arranged a weekend they would never forget. For the first time in their lives, these children saw tall buildings, rode in elevators, visited department stores and churches, ate ice cream in restaurants, stood with the motorman in streetcars. Even a house with a verandah was an object of interest.

A second-hand movie projector, operated by the battery from the Sloman's Model A Ford, introduced new wonders into the school car. Simple home movies borrowed from friends in Toronto were seen over and over again, and the sight of bicycles, children at play on streets, electric street lights, advertising billboards and common everyday scenes, helped to broaden their horizons.

A regular school day began early for the Slomans and never ended before 11 P.M. For many years evening classes were held for parents who were as anxious for an education as their children. Not only were they taught the "three Rs," these immigrant families were also given an insight into Canadian business affairs and the Canadian way of life. There were social evenings for the families with spelling games, Bingo, movies, general conversation and refreshments baked by Mrs. Sloman, to finish off the party-like affair.

So successful was the school-on-wheels project that two more cars were added in 1928, and by the late 1940s there were seven in operation, travelling thousands of miles in northern Ontario. There were four on CNR lines, two on CPR lines and one on the T.&N.O. Railway.

Every passing train saluted the red schoolhouse on wheels, and in 1939, when the Royal Train toured Canada, King George VI and Queen Elizabeth stopped off to say hello.

The Slomans raised their own five children on the school car, and educated them until they completed grade twelve. Their last year of high school was taken in their hometown high school in Clinton, Ontario. Joan went on to graduate in mathematics from Western University and holds her M.A.; Elizabeth entered medicine when she was just sixteen-and-a-half and is now a doctor; Margaret is a nurse, and the twins, Bill and Fredda, youngest members of the family, graduated in photographic arts from Ryerson in Toronto.

For the Ontario Department of Education it would have been impossible to find a more dedicated teacher than Fred Sloman. The life demanded complete unselfishness from him and his family. They had to be willing to forego the companionship

Fred Sloman and pupils, CN school car >

Fred Sloman and pupils outside the CN school car

of friends and relatives. There was no such thing as a weekend off. Laundry for seven Slomans was done by hand, and not until 1944 was there a bathtub in the school car. Winter came early and lasted half the year. Such conditions could have strained family relationships, but for the Slomans the entire experience was a happy one.

When he retired from the school on wheels in 1964, Fred Sloman's reward was knowing that his graduates were spread across Canada, many practicing law, medicine, nursing and teaching. Over 1,000 children had come out of the bush and graduated from the first "School on Wheels" in Ontario. Letters still come regularly to Mrs. Sloman from former pupils who will never forget their debt of gratitude to their first schoolteacher, the late Fred Sloman.

LONDESBOROUGH

Unless you have lived in Huron County, it's possible you've never been in Londesborough. It's just a small, pleasant, rural village. But 100 years ago, the London, Huron & Bruce Railway way "put it on the map." Four passenger trains stopped daily in the village, and the railroad built one of its largest stations for this farming community.

The village still exists, but the station and railway are gone; the railway which was once so familiar to everyone in Huron County, is seldom mentioned now. It was a short rural line running between London and Wingham, just seventy-four miles in all. Built with the help of the Great Western Railway in 1875, it became amalgamated with the Grand Trunk Railway in 1882, and in 1923 it became a part of the Canadian National System. Despite all the changes, it was always known as the London, Huron & Bruce. Trains with exotic names such as "The Flyer," or "The Express" never used this line. Speed really wasn't very important with the L.H. & B., and in fact, engineers would have had trouble trying to set speed records because there wasn't time to build up steam between station stops. Every farmer and villager who lived along the line of the L.H. & B. regarded the railway as a family affair right from the moment it was planned, and when service was finally concluded it was a sad day for them.

Construction of the London, Huron & Bruce was followed by the villagers with interest, and daily bulletins in local newspapers reported its progress. Excitement was aroused when the announcement was made stating, "Plans have been completed for the railway from London to Wingham. Coming through Londesborough, the tracks will run through the farms of Mr. Craven and Mr. Murdock."

Plans continued on schedule and in June 1875 another bulletin said, "Work is progressing so rapidly that there is every probability the trains will be running to Exeter, if not Clinton in three months." By November 6, 1875, the track laying was completed between London and Londesborough and "the work of ballasting the road is being pushed forward with vigor, and there is every probability of an early opening of the line for traffic."

Excitement was riding high all fall in Londesborough, and after the latter bulletin was published on November 10th, side roads were busy with farmers in buggies out to see the fun. It was reported that "A train with 17 cars arrived in Clinton on Wednesday, November 10th. The engine with cars has been up as far as Mr. Murdock's farm which is close to the village."

The last spike on the London, Huron & Bruce was driven in on Saturday, December 11, 1875, but the big celebration of the line's completion didn't take place until a month later. The wait was well worth it; the enthusiasm shown on that occasion is seldom seen today, and the front page of every local newspaper carried stories of the event. The London newspaper said:

The first passenger train left London at 5 minutes past two o'clock on Monday, January 11, 1876, having on board a delegation of the Celebrating Committee, and proceeded to Wingham for the purpose of conveying the guests to the banquet along the route to London. The entire number arriving at London being 700. On arriving at London, the excursionists were met at the depot by the General Commission and a large number of the citizens. In the city a scene of gaiety presented itself. Flags and banners were profusely exhibited, and at intervals the peals of St. Paul's chimes and the musical notes of the striking clock added to the effect. About 3 o'clock, the grand salute was fired by the men of Major Peters' Field Battery, the guns being in Victoria Park. The exhibition by the Fire Brigade gave a good deal of delight to the visitors, and served as the topic upon which to hinge many a remark, and form many opinions as to the relative advantages of steamers and hand-fired engines.

The banquet was in the evening. There were numerous speeches, and the guests returned by special trains provided for their accommodation by the Company on Wednesday morning, and reached their several destinations without mishap or accident having occurred to mar the pleasures of the trip, and all were loud in their praises of the kind treatment they had received at the hands of

LONDON TO WINGHAM.

TRAINS NORTH. **TRAINS SOUTH.**

THIRD CLASS. 75 Freight.	FIRST CLASS. 73 Passenger.	FIRST CLASS. 71 Passenger.	Miles from London.	STATIONS.	Miles from Wingham.	Te'graph Offices. D day	Te'graph Offices. N night	FIRST CLASS. 70 Passenger.	FIRST CLASS. 72 Passenger.	THIRD CLASS. 74 Freight.
P.M. 1.50	P.M. 8.00	A.M. **10.55**	74	ARR.....**Wingham**......DEP.		D		A.M. 7.00	P.M. 3.05	A.M. 10.30
1.45	**7.50**	**10.51**	73	........Wingham Junction....	1	D		7.03	**3.15**	a **10.40** d **11.15**
1.20	7.35	10.39	67¼	........Belgrave..............	6¾	D		7.17	3.29	11.38
12.50	7.20	10.24	60¾	........Blyth..................	13¼	D		7.32	3.44	P.M. 12.02
P.M. **12.17**	7.10	10.15	56¾	........Londesborough.........	17¼	D		7.41	3.53	**12.17**
11.50	6.55	10.00	....	........Clinton Junction..	....			7.55	4.07	12.37
11.45	6.50	9.55	50	........Clinton	24	D		8.03	4.13	1.00
10.55	6.40	9.50	....	........Clinton Junction.......	....			8.08	4.18	1.05
10.30	6.25	9.36	43¼	........Brucefield	30¾			8.22	4.32	1.25
10.12	6.13	9.29	39¼	........Kippen.................	34¾	D		8.31	4.40	1.40
10.00	6.05	9.24	37	........Hensall................	37	D		8.37	4.45	1.55
9.30 **8.35**	5.50	**9.14**	31¼	Dep. Arr. } **Exeter.** .... { Arr. Dep.	42¾	D		.... **8.51**	.... 5.00	2.12 2.30
8.10	5.35	**9.02**	26¼	........Centralia	47½	D		**9.02**	5.09	2.53
7.43	**5.20**	8.48	20¼	........Clandeboye	52½			9.16	**5.20**	3.20
....	5.15	8.43	18¾	........§Lucan Crossing	55¼			9.20	5.25	....
7.20	5.07	8.34	15¾	........Denfield...............	58¼	D		9.30	5.30	3.42
6.55	4.55	8.23	11¼	........Ilderton	62¾			9.41	5.38	4.04
....	4.46	8.15	7¾	........Ettrick................	66¼			9.50	5.45	....
6.20	**4.35**	8.05	4¼	........Hyde Park Junction...	69¾	D	N	10.00	5.50	**4.35**
6.05 A.M.	4.25 P.M.	7.55 A.M.	....	DEP....**London**........ ....ARR.	74	D	N	10.10 A.M.	6.00 P.M.	4.55 P.M.
75	73	71						70	72	74

London, Huron and Bruce Branch Trains must keep clear of all regular Main Line and Sarnia Branch Trains between Hyde Park and London, and must not start out from either London or Hyde Park without proper telegraph orders from the Superintendent through the Dispatcher; see Southern Division Time-Table for running of L. H. & B. Branch Trains between Hyde Park and London. L. H. & B. Branch Trains must also keep clear of all Kincardine Branch Trains between Wingham and Wingham Junction.

STRATFORD TO GODERICH.

TRAINS WESTWARD. **TRAINS EASTWARD.**

SECOND CLASS. 6 Mixed.	SECOND CLASS. 4 Mixed.	FIRST CLASS. 2 Passenger.	Miles from Stratford.	STATIONS.	Miles from Goderich.	Te'graph Offices. D day	Te'graph Offices. N night	FIRST CLASS. 1 Passenger.	SECOND CLASS. 3 Mixed.	SECOND CLASS. 5 Mixed.
P.M. 3.00	A.M. 10.40	P.M. 9.45	45.5	ARR.....**Goderich**........DEP.	....	D		A.M. 7.00	P.M. 12.15	P.M. 3.15
2.22	10.03	9.17	33.2	........Clinton Junction.......	12.3	D		7.24	12.50	3.48
2.20	10.00	9.15	32.6	........Clinton	12.9	D		7.30	1.05	a3.50 d4.15
1.48	9.00	8.57	24.5	........Seaforth...............	21.0	D		7.48	**1.48**	5.05
1.21	d **8.00** a **7.50**	8.44	18.0	........Dublin.................	27.0	D		**8.00**	2.20	5.35
1.00	7.25	8.30	12.8	........Mitchell...............	32.7	D		8.10	2.40	6.10
12.27	6.10	8.12	5.0	........Sebringville............	40.0			8.28	3.05	6.40
12.10 P.M.	5.50 A.M.	8.00 P.M.	....	DEP....**Stratford**........ARR.	45.0	D		8.40 A.M.	3.25 P.M.	7.00 P.M.
6	4	2						1	3	5

Any Train failing to arrive at Hyde Park Junction, Wingham, Stratford or Goderich on time, must keep clear of all Trains of a like or superior class that may be due to leave.—See Rules Nos. 48, 49 and 57. Diamond Crossing, Clinton Junction—See Rule No. 112. All regular trains will run daily, Sundays excepted. §No side tracks.

London, Huron & Bruce Railway timetable

the people, and feeling convinced that railway banqueting is not such a bad business after all.

Life in Londesborough began to move at a new pace when the L.H. & B. arrived, and after having been called Hagyard's Corners since its earliest days, it became Londesborough—a name with more class! New businesses were soon attracted to the village, and the four corners quickly expanded to hold a post office, grist mill, general store, four waggon shops, a church and a millinery shop. A buggy and sleigh maker also moved in, as did a barber, who gave a moustache cup to every customer. The most lively establishment was a hotel called "The Ploughboy," and a few doors from it was the Temperance Hall.

Londesborough's first railway station was a functional, frame building of board and batten design, and it served the community until 1907 when it was destroyed by fire. Mr. W. F. Mylne was its first station agent. A bad fire broke out in July 1881, threatening to level the building, but it was brought under control by the villagers. It was reported that "they carried water from the station pump, and when that gave out, it had to be brought from the river on the jigger." Londesborough was a wood-up station, and the great stacks of cordwood piled around the station frequently presented a fire hazard, particularly so on this occasion.

When a whole trainload of farm machinery arrived at the Londesborough station in June 1881, almost the entire town turned out to see the unloading process, which merited mention in the paper: "A busy scene took place at the Londesborough Station, in the delivery and loading up of some 25 mowing and reaping machines from the celebrated factory of D. Maxwell of Paris, under the superintendence of Mr. Maxwell Jr. and Mr. Trenamen and the agent, John Brundsdon of Londesborough. After all were loaded, they made a grand procession to the village where Mr. Bell (owner of the Ploughboy Hotel) provided a sumptuous repast for the entire company of about 50 people."

The Londesborough station had six different agents in its

sixty-five years. A Mr. Jeffrey followed Mr. Mylne in 1888 and stayed until 1904. Mr. Fawcett followed him, and then came Percy Carisle. He was the agent in 1907, the year the old station burned down. The cause of the fire was never discovered; one of its worst results was a heavy loss for apple buyers when flames spread to the freight sheds.

Building of the new station was postponed until spring, because of the very severe snowstorms that winter. Grand Trunk Railway, who now owned the L. H. & B., chose a design which was popular for their stations at that time.

In a long list of rules published by the Grand Trunk in 1898, agents and telegraphers had to work a 12-hour day with an hour for meals included. An agent and telegrapher on a branch line, at a station with dwelling, fuel and light, received the princely monthly wage of $35. However, if he did not have a company dwelling, his salary was increased to $40. There were fringe benefits for a telegrapher, which relieved him of some unpleasant duties: "He is not required to cut wood, load or unload wood or coal, sift ashes, clean or disinfect stock or other cars, or outbuildings. If telegraphers are required to attend switch lamps or semaphore lamps they will receive $3.00 per month per station for four or less of such lamps, and 50¢ per month for each additional switch or semaphore light at such station." It's doubtful that telegraphers ever became rich men, but their job was a popular one within the railway.

The second to last station agent at Londesborough was Will Lyon, who followed Mr. Carisle in 1909 and held the job for 15 years. Mr. Fred Thompson was the last station agent, and it was he who sold the last train tickets at the station when it closed on April 26, 1941.

On December 6, 1940, clerks of the municipalities bordering on the CNR right-of-way from Clinton to Wingham were advised that "action was being taken to close that portion of the road," and on April 26, 1941, service was discontinued.

"Sentimental Journey" would certainly have been an appropriate title for the farewell train ride. CNR's engine #1318, pulling train #603, steamed out of Wingham station,

tion in the coaches was quiet and reminiscent. Passengers recalled the nickname, "The Butter and Egg Special," given to the train in its early years. In those days farmers' wives all along the line had carried baskets of butter and eggs to sell at the market in London.

Wherever the train stopped that day, the station agent and members of the train crew shook hands with new and departing passengers. The entire event was similar to the break-up of closely-knit family. Newspapers made their final report of the last moments of the London, Huron & Bruce by saying, "there were no silk hats, flags or speeches to mark the occasion."

Blyth Station on the London, Huron & Bruce line

heading south for the last time. Mr. L. C. Steele, who had been on the run for ten years, was conductor that day, and his crew consisted of A. Sherlock, trainman; William Rowell, engineer; Roy Steinberg, expressman; and N. S. Fletcher and W. H. Acres, mail clerks.

The seats in the coaches were filled with passengers who had ridden on the train all their lives. There were old men on board who remembered when the railway was built, and they brought along their grandsons so that they could tell their own grandsons some day. At Belgrave, old "Bill," the horse that had always drawn the mail from the station, was standing in his usual spot, unaware that his job had come to an end. A crate of baby chicks was the last piece shipped on the line. Conversa-

Among lifelong residents of towns built along that famous old railway, the Ontario Simcoe and Huron Union Railway, now the CNR, there seems to be a definite pride when they discuss their railway. This is particularly apparent in the town of Stayner, Ontario, a few miles south of Collingwood on Georgian Bay (originally the terminus of this railway in 1855). When you talk to the former Reeve of Stayner, Mr. N. A. Oehm, and his son, Peter (president of the Upper Canada Railway Society), whose home is just a block away from the railway station, you are aware of their infectious enthusiasm for the railway's history. Another way that Stayner residents display their pride in the railway is their treatment of the town's old station. This little, frame building has retained its dignity even though it is in use by a Co-op. It has escaped the fate of many old stations, which have been crudely transformed for a variety of other purposes.

The Ontario Simcoe and Huron Union Railway (usually referred to as the "Oats, Straw, & Hay Railway"), was a long-awaited railway, and it caused more excitement in Ontario than had just about any other event up till that time. Its sod-turning ceremony took place in October 1851 with great pomp. Lady Elgin, wife of the Governor General, performed the honours. The first passenger train made its maiden journey on the line on May 16, 1853, going from Toronto to Machell's Corners (now known as Aurora). From that day, all communities north of Machell's Corners, right up to Collingwood, were in a fever of excitement waiting for the arrival of their first passenger train. The great day for Stayner and Collingwood was on January 1, 1855. There wasn't quite the same fanfare on this occasion as had been displayed earlier at the sod-turning ceremony, mainly because the rolling stock was rather humble in style. It would have been difficult for any newspaper reporter to write a glowing report about a train made up of a woodburning locomotive pulling a couple of open flatcars, with rough, board benches nailed to the floor and cedar boughs tacked at intervals along the sides, to add a dash of class. Nevertheless, it was the beginning of a new era, and settlers who had waited expec-

tantly for this exciting moment were confident of better days ahead. Stayner was known as Nottawasaga Station in the early days, and until the arrival of the railway it was not a community of any size or importance.

Property in the area had been bought up as early as 1836, but it was not put to use until rumours spread about the coming of a railway. Records show that John A. Macdonald of Kingston (later, Canada's first prime minister) had bought property in Stayner in 1854 and sold it a year later, at a tidy profit of just over two thousand dollars. (I wonder if he had to answer to the House for that!)

With the arrival of the railway, a busily humming village began to develop. Soon there were mills, a foundry, a great variety of shops, a weekly newspaper called *The Sun*, four hotels, one of which was called the Railway Hotel. (In those days, no railway town would dream of being without a Railway Street or Railway Hotel; they even made railway soap and railway suspenders!) There was a dentist on the main street whose mode of advertising sent chills of terror through its observers— a lifelike molar, complete with ugly roots, hung on a swinging sign outside his office.

The highlight of Stayner's railway history must surely have been in 1860, during the visit of the dashing young Prince of Wales, Albert Edward, son of Queen Victoria. Trains were still a novelty to most people at that time, and the appearance of the Royal Train must have been an unforgettable sight. Fred Cumberland, director of the railway (now known as the Northern Railway), was in charge of plans for festivities during the prince's visit, and for him the fitting theme was "elegance." Never before had Toronto, or any other Ontario community, seen such splendour. Bunting, banners, banquets and bands ensured that the royal trip would be without a single dull moment.

A special train was made up in Toronto to take the Prince of Wales on his first tour of the Northern Railway, and the train, of course, was subjected to a massive clean-up campaign. Its locomotives and coaches glistened with fresh paint, and brass bells and fittings shone like spun gold. The first open observation car ever built in Canada was used on this trip, adding the final touch of elegance.

Railway stations in every town along the route paid their respects to the prince with a mass of decorations. There were flags and garlands of cedar boughs garnishing the stations themselves, and colourful floral arches spanning the tracks. At the Stayner station there was not only a floral arch, but a bagpipe band which had been practicing for weeks for this occasion. The railway engineer had to slow his locomotive down almost to a standstill so that the prince could enjoy the stirring music.

The train's arrival in Collingwood must have startled even the prince, who by now was probably accustomed to all the splendour in his honour. At this town, the terminus of the Northern Railway, no less than twelve floral arches spanned the tracks, and an estimated crowd of 10,000 spectators cheered wildly when the Royal Train made its appearance.

In 1868, railways became quite style-conscious over their stations' appearances and sought to enhance their beauty with colourful gardens. To encourage station agents to beautify the station grounds, an annual prize was awarded to the agent who created the most outstanding effects. An attractive, white, picket fence erected around the late 1860s was one of Stayner's contributions to the general beautification campaign.

Near the station Stayner had a bell tower, which helped the town folk keep track of the hour, four times each day. Unfortunately the tower blew down during one particularly violent storm and the bell hit the railway tracks. The railway company attempted to repair the damage, but the once-musical bell lost its appealing tone in that accident. The young lad who had to go out in all kinds of weather, six days a week, to ring the town bell four times each day, obviously didn't belong to a bell ringers' union. It is recorded that his yearly salary was just $8.

Another familiar sight near the railway station was a huge windmill. Under it was the deep well that supplied water for the town fire department.

Like so many other towns, Stayner had a problem with cattle that roamed the streets; they were drawn to the railway tracks by their inordinate fondness for the lush grass that grew along the right-of-ways. (Its lushness was attributable to the potash and other minerals that were the residue from coal-burning locomotives.) Train crews had to take their trains through town at a snail's pace in order to avoid hitting the cattle and, in time, they came to refer to Stayner as "Cow Town." Eventually a by-law was passed, forbidding people to allow their cattle the run of the town.

If ever a town loved a parade, it was Stayner. There were the usual ones, expected on national or patriotic holidays and, of course, a Santa Claus parade too, but there were three others which had a definite "frontier town" flavour, and these three were attended with great enthusiasm by almost everyone. Horse Day was held once a month. It occurred after a horse dealer had spent a month lining up and buying enough horses to fill a railway boxcar. On the big day, all the horses would be brought into town and stabled for a day at a livery. Before train time, people would line the streets to see the string of about twenty or more horses jogging down Main Street to the train station. Canny observers became quite proficient in being able to detect tell-tale signs which indicated whether the horse dealer had been "taken" on a deal.

Once a year a farm-implement dealer would tour the countryside taking orders from farmers for the latest in farm equipment; the date of the delivery would be settled for early spring. No sideshow was ever prepared with greater thought than this event. Letters were sent out to each farmer reminding him of the big day in the offing, and telling him to leave his horse and rig at the livery behind one of the hotels in town. At noon, farmers were treated to a fine fifty-cent dinner at the best hotel, and their thirst would be appeased in the hotel's bar. Following this popular ritual (the bills all footed by the implement company, of course), the farmers collected their new farming equipment at the station and, preceded by the town band, they paraded the full length of main street with their spick-and-span new equipment.

There was a degree of decorum to the implement parade, but the Stock Day parade was a different matter. All during the week drovers scoured the countryside buying hogs, and on Saturday these animals were herded into town and corralled until train time. Just before the train was due in it was considered fair game for young lads and older men to make something of a game of driving the hogs to the tracks. They used branches, whips, etc. — anything to give the animal a sense of direction. This parade of hogs and drivers went down Main Street, but there was definitely an absence of refinement to the affair. On one occasion, a sow dashed into a drygoods shop, made a rapid tour of the aisles and hustled out dragging a pair of bloomers.

An interesting discovery was made at the station several years ago when carpenters were dismantling a wall in the freight shed. When the plaster was torn away from the laths, out rolled scores of empty liquor bottles. Many were almost as old as the station! One of the early station employees apparently had two problems: his insatiable thirst, and how to dispose of the evidence. He solved the latter by reaching up to an opening in the top of the partition, and dropping the bottles out of sight.

Saturdays in towns like Stayner produced a constant scene of action in those early days. The grand finale on every Saturday night seemed to be reserved unofficially for the young, unmarried set. At 9 P.M. they arrived at the station en masse to see the night train go through. On Sunday evenings after church service, the ritual was repeated.

It's all changed now. There are no night passenger trains — in fact, no passenger trains at any time. Occasionally the Upper Canada Railway Society organizes a steam excursion train trip, which explores the line of the historic Ontario Simcoe and Huron Union Railway, which went through Stayner in 1855. On the 125th anniversary of the completion of the old railway line — which eventually went right on to Meaford — another railway excursion will be scheduled. Already, towns are planning celebrations for the event, and the town of Stayner expects to have its gardens a mass of bloom, as they were in the early years. Bands will be playing and, no doubt, a bagpipe band will be on hand when the train comes to a halt at the lovely, old, railway station.

HOG BAY TRESTLE

The Hog Bay railway trestle is gone, torn down timber by timber in the winter of 1977. But it still exists as long as there are a few old railwaymen around who can remember being at the throttle of a powerful CPR steam locomotive, hauling a string of grain cars from Canada's prairies, and cautiously inching the precious cargo over the rails of the trestle. And in the memories of men who were venturesome boys in the early part of this century the trestle still stands. When they get together they swap yarns about the days they scrambled up the embankment to the tracks and ran breathlessly over the ties, hoping they wouldn't be caught.

No sideshow ever drew a more appreciative audience than the old wooden trestle, and it didn't cost a cent for a front-row seat. For over half a century it provided the answer to that timeless question, "What will we do today?" Kids pedaled there on their bikes after school, and entire families drove out, to make a day of watching long freights and passenger trains crossing at the prescribed 5 miles per hour. It was a real thrill to stand below the trestle, feeling the vibrating timbers as locomotives laboured up the incline at the north end. But for the most spectacular view of it and the countryside for miles around, you climbed halfway up the hill across the highway. From there, distant trains could be seen heading for the trestle, like long smoking serpents moving away from the grain elevators. Behind particularly long trains would be an extra engine which provided the train with sufficient power to get up the long approach to the trestle. Those exciting shows came to an end when steam locomotives were taken off in 1956. The last time any train ever made the crossing was in March 1971. Safety tests proved that the trestle was just not built for the heavy, new diesel trains.

Residents of the neighbouring communities, Midland, Victoria Harbour and Waubaushene, became uneasy when the CPR demolished the southern approach to the trestle. It appeared that the beloved old structure was doomed. "Save the trestle" committees were formed, but their appeals were turned down. The cost of maintaining the unused bridge would be

phenomenal they were told, and rotting timbers were already creating a hazard for children who raced across the unprotected tracks. Surprised wreckers found it was no easy task to dismantle the bridge, but by Christmas 1977 all that remained of this famous old landmark was a wooden skeleton swaying giddily over frozen Hog Bay.

It all began back in 1909, when the CPR was looking for a shorter route to the east coast for their rail and steamship operations. They chose a site on Georgian Bay, across from Victoria Harbour, and called it Port McNichol in honour of one of their vice presidents. A deep harbour was dredged, grain elevators lined the waterfront and two handsome railway stations were built. It was another example of a town being built around the railway. When track construction reached Hog Bay, the simplest way to reach the other side appeared to be by spanning it. And that's just what they did.

No bridge was ever constructed in a more unorthodox fashion, but even today the results would have satisfied the critical eye of any inspector. Mike McPeake, a man of few words, was the contractor, and his knowledge of bridge construction was gained locally from experience. He didn't have to see his plans on paper; they were clearly fixed in his head. This remarkable man knew exactly how the bridge should be built and how it would appear upon completion. Old-timers who watched the progress of the trestle still recall Mike's casual method of calculating and measuring the required material. When every carpenter and labourer had been briefed for the day, Mike could be seen hiking down the road in the direction of Victoria Harbour, where he quenched the thirst he had built up. The completed bridge was a handsome geometrical structure, artistically, a gem, and it was capable of carrying with ease years of heavy rail traffic.

Port McNichol became the home port of CPR's fleet of three Great Lakes passenger and freight boats: the S.S. Assiniboia, the S.S. Keewatin and the S.S. Manitoba. These ships plied between Port McNichol, Sault Ste. Marie, Port Arthur and Fort William, carrying freight during the April to

December navigation season, and operating as a passenger service from June until early September. The trip became so well-liked that the same passengers would return year after year. A special boat train brought them up from Toronto to Port McNichol, where they stepped out onto a flower-covered wharf that served CP's elegant, white ships. It was sheer luxury all the way. For most people, the highlight of the train trip was crossing the 2,141-foot-long wooden trestle over Hog Bay. The imposed slow rate of speed prolonged the thrill of sitting in a railway coach suspended high over the water.

All CP's engineers who shuttled back and forth over the Hog Bay Trestle are retired pensioners now. When they get together to recall the old days, stories are rehashed and relived, no doubt gaining a bit in colour with the telling. The late Alf Bunker never forgot the terrifying moment when the front wheels of his locomotive, a CP 2300, derailed when he was taking 80 empty grain cars over the bridge into the port. Until that time he had never been disturbed by the distance between the top of the bridge and the water. That day it looked black and threatening and, in his imagination, he could almost feel the locomotive toppling over the edge. There was no way for him to get out onto the single track; he just had to wait for help to come. It was the only derailment in the history of the trestle.

Herb Stitt, a retired CPR engineer, still shudders at the memory of the wintry night he foolishly decided to walk back to Port McNichol after spending the evening with friends in Victoria Harbour. The ice on the bay seemed solid enough underfoot when he started out, but before long he became aware of its instability. The great angular trestle silhouetted against the night sky served as a guide, but blowing snow confused his sense of direction and reduced visibility to just a few feet. When the north end of the trestle eventually loomed up, right in front of him, Mr. Stitt had a new respect for the old landmark.

During both World Wars there was a constant threat of sabotage to the Hog Bay Trestle. The Canadian army posted armed guards at both ends and hourly patrols were made over the rails— not an enviable walk during the frequent blizzards which blew in from Georgian Bay!

But the old trestle is gone now. Soon, only the plaque erected by the roadside will remind us that here stood an historic railway bridge. Although Canada was over twenty years behind England and the United States in her development of the railway, she still made many important contributions to the industry and created several "firsts." When the CPR built its wooden railway trestle over Hog Bay it became the longest one of its kind in North America.

Roy Lunau, CPR roundhouse foreman, Owen Sound

OWEN SOUND CPR ROUNDHOUSE

What could be more desolate than an abandoned railway roundhouse? It takes a lot of searching now to find a roundhouse anywhere, and yet a few years ago they were a common sight in towns throughout the province. When steam locomotives were being replaced by diesel trains in the late 1950s, the familiar roundhouse vanished too — practically unnoticed. It seems that diesel locomotives don't need the care and protection of the roundhouse and can sit outside unattended while not in use. In fact, their motors are seldom turned off. But a steam locomotive, finished for the day, was moved to the ash pit for cleanout with just enough steam remaining to fuel its way into the roundhouse.

At the Canadian Pacific Railway's terminus in Owen Sound, it's still possible to see a frame roundhouse, typical of the design used in the late 1800s. However, it's doubtful that it will remain much longer. This roundhouse, with its twenty-foot-high doors at each of the five entrances, is a relic of one of Ontario's pioneer railways, the Toronto, Grey and Bruce, which opened in June 1873 and was taken over by the CPR in 1884.

Roy Lunau, the only employee at the Owen Sound roundhouse, carries the title of "chargeman." He used to have crews working around the clock, servicing locomotives from the frequent passenger trains, grain trains and yard engines. Now the only traffic entering this once-busy rail yard is the way-freight from Orangeville on its thrice-weekly visit.

It's a depressing place to see today. Remnants of unused equipment from another era gather dust where they hang on the walls. The five, empty train stalls are permanently stained by smoke and oil, and although a steam locomotive hasn't been in the roundhouse for at least twenty years, the atmosphere is still pungent. The ventilators (called "jacks") removed most of the fumes from the pits, but any old railwayman will tell you that nothing in this world can totally remove the wonderful aroma left behind by a steam locomotive.

Roy Lunau uses the same office and equipment provided for chargemen in 1890. Business is conducted from an indestructible roll-top desk and caboose chair. Memos are still typed out on an ancient typewriter that undoubtedly would be treasured by any museum.

Hand-operated turntables, such as the one outside the Owen Sound roundhouse, are probably scarcer than round-houses. Despite its vintage, lack of use and the crop of weeds pushing up between the ties, the turntable still operates with clockwork ease. Eighty-year-old Herbert Stitt, retired CPR engineer, always associates the turntable and roundhouse with the weariness he felt when bringing in his locomotive after gruelling hours spent in the unforgettable storms in 1944. Storms are legendary in this snowbelt area around Owen Sound, and back then it was not uncommon for a three-hour trip to stretch into days. The arrival at the roundhouse meant the promise of much-needed sleep for exhausted crews.

Owen Sound's railway history began in 1873 when the Toronto, Grey and Bruce Railway extended its line from Orangeville to Owen Sound, thus completing the line to Georgian Bay. This section was called the Grey Extension and was opened for traffic on August 9 of that year. For the sake of economy the Toronto, Grey and Bruce was a narrow gauge railway measuring 3'6" rather than 5'6", which was the more popular gauge in Canada at that time. However, when the standard gauge in all of North America became 4'8½" in 1878, it was agreed that this railway should comply. Due to the company's critical financial situation in that period, the change did not take place until December 1881. The railway was leased to the Ontario, Quebec Railway in 1883, and to the Canadian Pacific Railway in 1884. Its addition to CPR's operation was of great importance because it completed the all-Canadian route to the west by rail and water. (CP's rails were still incomplete around the north shore of Lake Superior.) A steamship service was established in 1884 between Port Arthur and Owen Sound, providing a fast route for the shipment of grain from the Canadian west. This service was called "The Thunder Bay Route" and was in effect until 1909. At that time the CPR, looking for a still-shorter route to the eastern seaboard for its grain trains,

CPR locomotive on hand-operated turntable

moved the entire operation to Port McNichol, a harbour they dredged on Georgian Bay, not far from Midland. This was a sad blow to the town, and the event touched off the decline of Owen Sound's importance as a rail and shipping centre on the Great Lakes. CP's two grain elevators were destroyed by fire in 1911 and never rebuilt. The bunkhouse disappeared soon after steam locomotives were taken off the line, and gradually all freight sheds, tool shacks, etc., were demolished too. Oddly enough, a new railway station was built in 1970, the year CPR removed its passenger service from the line.

When they tear down the old roundhouse, visible evidence of the Toronto, Grey and Bruce's history will be practically erased. Few pioneer railways contributed so much colour to Canadian railway history. It had the famous Fairlie locomotive called the "Caledon" — a freak in design with its two boilers joined back to back by a single firebox that divided the cab of the locomotive. All topped-off by two enormous smoke-stacks, the sight never failed to intrigue spectators. The T.G.&B. was also well-known in the area for its annual railway Pic-Nics. Tragedy marred the company's history in September 3, 1907, at the infamous "Horseshoe Curve" on the line near Caledon. A special holiday train was derailed there, killing seven passengers.

Railway enthusiasts frequently band together to prevent the destruction of historic railway stations, and it's certain they will be heard from when the roundhouse is to be demolished. The possibilities for new uses of old railway stations are endless, but what can be done with a roundhouse? CPR's Owen Sound roundhouse is certainly not beautiful, but it's the last one in rural Ontario and one of the final ties with the vanished Steam Era. It will be a sad day when it goes.

"So who needs a railway?" That was the contention of its opponents in Prince Edward County during the 1870s. In a region surrounded by water, with a prosperous shipbuilding industry and an export trade handled through its harbours, a railway hardly seemed necessary. Moreover, all of the county's transportation needs were taken care of by the reliable stagecoach service that connected with the Grand Trunk Railway in Belleville, or by the steamship service that ran between Picton, Belleville and Kingston.

But strong Tories were convinced that this progressive county could no longer afford to ignore the railway. After all, almost every other county in Canada West had been building lines feverishly since 1853. The Grand Trunk had been running passenger trains between Montreal and Toronto since 1854; Cobourg had built its controversial line over Rice Lake to Peterborough; Port Hope had one going right up to Beaverton on Lake Simcoe; Prescott and Brockville both had lines. In fact, railway maps of Canada West of the 1870s looked like vast spider webs.

Its indifference to the railway was an example of the independent spirit of this historic county, located at the northeast corner of Lake Ontario. It had been settled by Loyalists who fled from the revolution of the British Colonies in North America, between 1775 and 1883. The thousand original settlers who came to Prince Edward County were from disparate backgrounds, but they were united in their loyalty to the crown and in their desire to live quietly and peacefully.

History reveals that these settlers had long-range plans for establishing a permanent place for themselves in the county, and by the 1860s they had taken up all the land. Their loyalty to the crown is demonstrated by the names they chose for their villages and townships. The county's name was in honour of Prince Edward, son of George III, who became the father of Queen Victoria. Sophiasburg, Ameliasburgh, Marysburgh, Adolphustown, Ernestown—all were named after members of the royal family.

Without the assistance of a railway, Prince Edward County enjoyed the greatest prosperity in its history between the years of 1869 and 1890. These were the "Barley Years." The soil of the county produced the best malting barley available, and distillers in the United States purchased all that could be grown. County-built schooners shipped out millions of tons of barley, ranging in price from seventy cents to one dollar a bushel, before protesting United States farmers forced Congress to impose an embargo on foreign imports in 1890.

When the railway was finally introduced into the county, railway building had slowed down considerably in other parts of Canada. After the railway surveyed a line to run between Trenton and Picton, a sod-turning ceremony took place in 1873. That ended all activity until 1878 when actual construction began. The 32-mile railway was formally opened on October 27, 1879, and was called the Prince Edward County Railway. Its meagre rolling stock consisted of two wood-burning locomotives, "The Picton" and "The Trenton," two wooden coaches, two baggage cars and two flatcars. The company changed hands in 1881, and the first task of the new owners, the McMullen Brothers, was to change the location of Picton's railway station. Through poor planning, the station had been built outside the town's boundary at Sandy Hook. A new location was chosen on Lake Street, in the heart of town, and a crowd of curious spectators was on hand to watch the station being installed. Preparations for the move appeared to be snag-free, but the actual event was plagued with problems. The station had to be cut in half to be loaded onto railway flatcars, and as the cavalcade began moving down the tracks it met an immovable object, the barn of a Mr. Crandall. The station sections projected out too far beyond the tracks to allow the train to pass, and after much head scratching it was decided to chop off a corner of the barn. The train with its unwieldy cargo then proceeded without further delay.

This first railway station in Picton was a simple two-story frame building, dressed up with gables on all four sides. It was replaced early in the 1900s with a handsome, red-brick station which still stands today, although it is not in use as a passenger

Picton Station, moved approx. 1 mile from Sandy Hook to Picton in 1891

PICTON STATION
Prince Edward County Railway 1889

station. Traffic along the line was never brisk, and no doubt this misfortune caused the minority Grits of the county who had always opposed the construction of the railway to rub their hands with glee. The Canadian Northern Railway took over the ailing company in 1909, and in 1919, it was absorbed by the Canadian National Railway. The Picton railway station was offered for sale in 1975, and is presently owned by a lumber firm.

Fortunately, not all the county's ventures in transportation failed. Up until recent years Picton's harbour was a busy lake-shipping port and is still a popular haven for Great Lakes' summer sailors. William Weller, owner of Upper Canada's most famous stagecoach line, "The Royal Mail Line," was born in

the county at Carrying Place. A speed record was established in the winter of 1840 by his company when Lord Sydenham, Governor-in-Chief of Canada, needed to make a hasty visit to Montreal, from Toronto, so that he could order a reprieve for a convict sentenced to hang. William Weller, known as "King of the stage coach proprietors," personally drove the coach, and it completed the 360-mile trip in the incredible time of just thirty-five hours and forty minutes.

Sir John A. Macdonald (long before he became Canada's first prime minister) played a minor role in the county's railway history. But he is probably better remembered for some of the early events of his law career in Picton, where he fought his first court case in 1834. Still more colourful was his first

CNR station

encounter with the law, following a prank one winter night. He and some friends discovered a dead horse lying frozen stiff on the main street of Picton. Together, they hauled the carcass along to the Methodist chapel and placed it in a sitting position in the pulpit with its feet on the lectern's edge. The resulting scandal can only be imagined!

Travellers exploring the towns and back roads of Prince Edward County are acutely aware of the presence of those early settlers, the United Empire Loyalists. The serenity they sought when they settled the county exists there today. Descendants of those first families are still regarded as the "first families" of the county. Isolated points along the shore recall the memory of sailing ships that were lost in storms, long ago, before light-houses were erected to warn ships of the hazardous rocks. Two rusting railway tracks winding through the countryside, passing through Carrying Place, Hillier, Wellington, Bloomfield and halting in Picton, recall the hundred-year-old Prince Edward County Railway which wasn't really needed.

KINMOUNT

Canada's "Kings" in the 1800s were the lumber kings. Some started out humbly, with only a few hundred acres of timberland, while others were able to afford thousands of acres. They built roads, mills, hotels, factories and the town itself. One "King" even built his own railway!

Timber in unlimited quantities had drawn these men into sparsely settled, undeveloped sections of Ontario, but the stumbling block was lack of transportation. When Victoria County became aware of its virtually untapped wealth in lumber and iron, the urgent need for a railway was recognized. The Lindsay, Fenelon Falls and Ottawa Railway was chartered in 1872 — a line which would be built between Lindsay and Haliburton. At the time of the sod-turning ceremony in Lindsay, in August 1874, the railway's name had been changed to the Victoria Railway. It took almost three years to complete the first twenty-eight miles of this short railway and another two years to complete the line into Haliburton Village. On November 26, 1878, the entire line was officially opened.

Written into the history of every railroad in the early days was the familiar complaint, "financial difficulties." The Victoria Railway was no exception. A $20,000 railway bridge had to be built at Fenelon Falls to span the Otonabee River, and long stretches of rock had to be dynamited before the tracks reached Kinmount. Construction came to a halt at this point on the line until 1877, when the provincial government and the Canada Land and Emigration Company provided sufficient funds for continuation of the work.

Labour in the Kinmount area was done by a large group of Icelanders who had been brought in for that purpose and with the intention that they would remain as settlers. Illness struck their camp; wages were poor and slow in coming. Finally, in complete disillusionment with the railway and the community, the entire colony moved out and headed for Manitoba.

Despite its financial problems, the Victoria Railway was able to build handsome railway stations. Its most outstanding was the head office in Lindsay, a one-story red-brick building, which was known as the "union" station in town because its facilities were also used by the Whitby, Port Perry and Lindsay Railway.

For the sake of economy, however, other stations along the line, right up to Haliburton, were wooden and fairly standard in design. A characteristic touch was the high gables above the bay windows of the station operator's office. Generally, the colour used for these vertical, board and batten buildings was the favourite "boxcar red." Kinmount's station was built in the centre of the village close to the Burnt River, which frequently goes on a spring rampage. On May 24, 1928 it flooded its banks and covered the streets with two feet of water. Passengers had to be paddled to the station in canoes. This was the first event of exciting proportions since the night of the disastrous fire in 1890. It got under way one night when most of the villagers were congregated in the Baptist Church to hear a temperance lecture, and before the flames were under control, half the town had been levelled. Fire fighters brought up by train from Lindsay saved the village from being entirely wiped out.

Victoria County's railway history was one of "famine or feast." By the late 1870s, no less than four railways were running through the county. The Port Hope, Lindsay & Beaverton Railway arrived in Lindsay in October, 1857, then built an extension to Beaverton on Lake Simcoe. The Toronto and Nipissing, a narrow gauge railway 3'6" wide, was next to come along and was completed in the fall of 1872. It ran from Toronto to Coboconk, a distance of eighty-seven miles. The shortest line of all, the Whitby, Port Perry and Lindsay Railway, was supposed to plunge right on to the west coast of Canada, but on July 31, 1877, when forty-five miles of it had been completed, the enthusiasm ran out. It was nip and tuck throughout the entire construction of that little line, and in years to come the railway was always known as the "Nip and Tuck." The final railway to make its appearance in the county was the Victoria, fifty-six miles long, formally opened for traffic on November 26, 1878.

For Bud Mansfield, present operator at the Kinmount

station, the railway has been a family affair since its earliest days and has a special meaning. Bud's grandfather worked on the construction of the line, had timber rights along the line and sold wood for the wood-burning locomotives. Also, he was the builder of the original Kinmount station. Before the highways were kept open in winter, trains were the only form of transportation in the county and three passenger trains a day provided it with excellent service.

Each one of the pioneer railways which opened up Victoria County was bought by the Midland Railway of Canada in 1882, which in turn became consolidated with the Grand Trunk in 1893, ending up as a part of the CNR in 1923. That great era is finished. The lumber kings are gone, passenger trains vanished in the 1950s and all traffic is now handled by an occasional way-freight.

MAPLE

It was one of those bleak winter days when the fight for survival must hardly have seemed worthwhile. Every train was late; the driving wind had piled drifts of snow half-way up the bay window in front of the station operator's desk; passengers coming and going from the platform let in icy blasts of air each time the storm door swung open into the waiting room, and the potbelly stove which could usually be coaxed to a white-hot heat was barely taking the chill off the draughty old station.

For Charles Henry Byam, station agent-operator in Grand Trunk's Maple station in 1897, and for his wife and young children who lived in the railway cottage behind the station, that particular winter day would never be forgotten.

Railway families who lived in quarters above a station, or in an adjacent cottage provided for their use by the railway, were usually quite imperturbable people. A fast freight train, rumbling along just a few feet from bedroom windows, rattling every dish, pot and pan in the house, never disturbed the sleep of a railwayman's family. The shunting of boxcars, ringing train bells and shrill steam whistles were as much a part of the sounds of their home as the ticking clock. But let one variation occur in the familiar sounds, and the entire family would be wide-awake and up at the windows. So, when the through train to North Bay made an unscheduled stop at the Maple station on that blustery winter day, everyone sensed trouble.

The train was still moving when the conductor pulled open the coach door, shouting to Mr. Byam that a very sick lady was on board and they were bringing her in. Her anguish was sufficient indication that the birth of a child was imminent. Trainmen supported her across the snow-covered platform, and even in her distress she still held onto the hand of her bewildered three-year-old daughter. One of the passengers followed, carrying the young woman's only piece of luggage, a shabby wicker grip. The youngest Byam child was sent hurriedly off to bring back "Granny," the town's midwife, but before they could reach the cottage a baby girl had been born.

The unfortunate woman told her story a few hours later. She had been trying to reach her husband who was critically ill with tuberculosis in a Northern Ontario hospital. In his absence she had had to support herself and child, but when money ran out, in desperation, she decided to make the trip. There was just enough money for a one-way ticket. Her greatest concern now was the fear that the railway would no longer honour the ticket.

The story of her predicament was soon the talk of every family in Maple, and within hours bundles of baby clothes had been brought to the station. Although the cottage was only twenty-four by thirty feet, and just barely adequate for the Byam family, space was somehow found for the three unexpected guests and their gifts.

After two weeks of compassionate care, the young mother felt ready to continue her journey but hesitated to take along her new baby. Because her intention was to return to Toronto after a few days' visit with her husband, the Byams persuaded her to leave the baby with them for that short time. She and her older daughter were put on the North Bay morning train, and a ticket for the return trip tucked in her purse. The usual waving and calling back and forth went on while the train pulled away from the station — the Byams never saw her again.

Charles Byam and his wife were certain she would return, but months passed without a word from her. All efforts to find her failed. Occasionally an envelope would come in the mail with a few dollars tucked inside and a note assuring them of her hope to be back soon. The postmark was always from a different town. Eventually the letters stopped.

It seemed as though every family in Maple had an affectionate claim to this child. When it was realized that probably she would always be with them, she was christened, and almost everyone in town attended the church service. They called her "Maple."

LAKEFIELD

"Toonerville Trolley" was a favourite name for rural branch lines, and the incredibly slow, mixed train which meandered down the track was called "the flyer." The farmer's wife, or school children wanting a ride into town had only to wave their handkerchieves to bring the train to a halt at any crossroads.

These short lines, all built around one hundred years ago, had much in common: most operated in a relaxed manner, with company rules adjusted by employees to fit the situation of the moment, and all were the very lifeblood of the communities they served. It was considered fair game for villagers to poke fun at their own quaint railways, but if an outsider took the liberty of criticizing certain eccentricities, he would be properly put in his place.

Lakefield is at the end of one of these branch lines. In 1970, when it was rumoured that the town's railway station was to be demolished, the entire citizenry stood behind the quickly-grouped "Save Our Station" committee — and they won their battle! Passenger service into Lakefield had ended by 1970, but because the station had such poignant memories for almost everyone in town, the thought of its removal was shocking — almost a threat to the structure of the heritage, of which the residents were, and are, extremely proud.

This historic town was first surveyed in 1818 and named Nelson's Falls after its first settler, John Nelson. The community changed names four times before "Lakefield" was chosen, when the town was laid out in 1850. Among its best-known settlers were Samuel Strickland and his famous sisters, Catherine Parr Traill and Susanna Moodie, who arrived in the 1830s. They raised large families and yet still found time to record their experiences of life as early settlers. Today their writings are regarded as the most complete, factual source of research material on early pioneer life in Ontario.

Settlers in Peterborough County began pressing for better roads or a railway in the 1830s, and the town of Peterborough, just a short distance from Lakefield, succeeded in getting a line in 1857. Lakefield was not as fortunate though and had to wait until 1871. It was the Midland Railway of Canada which finally

built a short line into the town. (This pioneer railway was later consolidated with the old Grand Trunk.) To reach Lakefield you caught a train in Port Hope, which followed a line up to Millbrook Junction. At this station the line divided, with one track going on to Lindsay and the other cutting off to Peterborough, where you made your connection to Lakefield. The mixed train (passenger coaches and baggage car) joggled along for about three-quarters of an hour and eventually deposited you on the platform of Lakefield's fine, old, red-frame station.

The distance between Peterborough and Lakefield appears to have been debatable back then. A Midland Railway timetable, issued in May 1872, recorded it as being nine miles. A few years later, the Grand Trunk had it stretched out to eleven miles on their timetable. One hundred years later though, in 1977, when the Queen's Jubilee Train excursion took place on this branch line, a reporter for the local newspaper spoke of the distance as being just ten miles. Despite the confusion, the train had four legitimate stops to make in the short distance, which explains the reason why ten miles an hour was probably top speed. A train leaving Peterborough at 1:45 P.M. stopped ten minutes later at Hilliard's Junction. Four minutes later it steamed into Hazlitt's Junction where it stayed for thirteen minutes. Then it continued to Ashburn Mills, then Nassau Mills, finally Lakefield, and on to the turntable.

Shortly after the line was finished, Lakefield became a popular town with Peterborough organizations for their annual train excursions and "Pic-Nics." Occasionally, the mode of transportation for passengers on these informal outings was a boxcar decorated with cedar boughs, and the floor covered with hay. A piper, or band, at the station added to its festive air upon the arrival of these special trains.

The Lakefield branch line played an important role not only in the settling of the community, but also in the development of the Kawartha Lakes. For many years, during the summer months, the Friday night train would be packed with travellers heading off to resorts and cottages. The Stoney Lake Navigation Company installed a steamboat service in 1883 to

52

meet trains at the wharf and carry passengers on the rest of their journey.

The Trent Valley Navigation Company of Bobcaygeon also had a small fleet which travelled the full ninety miles of the Kawartha Lakes. In the company's brochure, published around the turn of the century, the voyage was described as covering a "90 mile stretch of limpid water." Author of the book, Edward Miller, used the flowery language popular among travel writers of his era to lure readers to the wonders of the Kawarthas. He wrote that "the Ogemah, speedy side-wheeler, has daily trips between Bobcaygeon and Burleigh Falls, down the great expanse of Lake Katchewanooka to Lakefield between the deep forest lining the water's edge on one hand, while on the other rise the feathered songsters as they dash hither and thither in countless numbers." In his description of Lakefield, Mr. Miller claimed that because of its elevation of 900 feet above sea level, it "insures the purest air, redolent with life-giving perfume borne on the balsam-laden breezes from the pinelands of the north, invigorating the system and refreshing wearied faculties."

The Stoney Lake Navigation Company had four steam-boats to handle the constant stream of summer passengers. The "Empress," the "Majestic," the "Stoney Lake" or the "Manita" would be on hand to meet each train.

Travellers holidaying in Lakefield were taken to either the Royal or Globe Hotel by a horse-drawn carry-all which was always backed up to the station at train time. Another familiar sight at the station was William "Billy" Stabler and his team of white horses. They pulled the express waggon around town for thirty-six years. "Billy" operated this delivery service until he was in his eighties and they say he was never late for a train.

Any Lakefield resident who has spent his entire life in the town has his own collection of memories of the old Grand Trunk branch line from Peterborough. Mrs. Winnifred Lampman recalls a trip which could only happen on a branch line. She had arrived on the Grand Trunk's "glamour" train of the day, "the Chicago Flyer," which stopped to allow her to transfer to the Peterborough mixed-train for the next leg of the journey. The fiercest storm of the winter had piled deep drifts along the line, creating havoc with train schedules. After several hours they eventually arrived in Peterborough, long after the Lakefield night train had departed. The prospect of spending the night on hard, railway-station benches was most unappealing to Mrs. Lampman and her companion, Elsie Ogilvie. A half-hour later, a locomotive, pulling a single wooden coach, puffed into the station. It was a private train, put on especially for two girls who had missed their connection. Perhaps Grank Trunk officials would have frowned at this gesture, but it did prove that chivalry was still very much alive in 1918.

A frequent passenger on the line who managed to get by without a ticket was "Tory," an Irish terrier. No one knew whom Tory visited, but frequently he got an urge to travel and would take the morning train to Peterborough. Some people were convinced that Tory could read a timetable because he was never late for a train. Occasionally his trips kept him over-night in Peterborough, and eventually he didn't come home again. His owner concluded that Tory must have become tired of his vagabond life and decided to stay in the big city, which seemed to have more appeal for him than town life.

It's certain that Lakefield must miss the life which came to town over the hundred-year-old branch line. Just one passenger train has been along in the past twenty years. Gone, too, are those marvellous old side-wheeler steamboats whose whistles competed with the arrival of every Grand Trunk train. The Port Hope, Lindsay and Beaverton, the Midland, the Grand Trunk—all were big names when they belonged to this little line, but they are found only in history books today. The line itself is neglected now and sadly resembles an elderly gentleman who is no longer useful to himself or his town.

Barry's Bay water tower

BARRY'S BAY AND MADAWASKA

"I saw the first train come into Barry's Bay in 1894 on the old O.A.&P.S. railway . . . yes, and I rode on the very first one that went on down to Madawaska." Probably no one else can make those statements today. For Thomas Patrick Murray of Barry's Bay, born on January 10, 1880, it seems like only yesterday that it all happened. The train he rode wasn't much of a train, he recalled, just a wooden coach and a couple of boxcars being pulled by a wood-burning locomotive. But it was the coach which impressed Mr. Murray; the seats were so soft — not the slat seats used on some of the earlier trains in Ontario. Swept up with enthusiasm for the railway, he got a job as water-boy with "old-Mackie," the sub-contractor, and earned fifty cents a day.

The Ottawa, Arnprior & Parry Sound Railway, usually called "The O.A.&P.S.," was built by Ontario's most ambitious lumberman, J. R. Booth. Ontario had many lumber kings in the early days, but J. R. Booth was recognized as "The Lumber King," or the "Lumber Baron," and his accomplishments proved he earned those titles. If his parents had known that their sickly child would be alive and still working at the age of ninety-nine they would have been astonished. Booth had a passionate fondness for doughnuts, and gave them credit for his longevity.

J. R. Booth's kingdom was based in Ottawa, and extended westerly through the Algonquin Highlands and on to Parry Sound where it connected with his shipping enterprise. It was estimated that in his Ottawa mills in 1870 he employed 2,000 men, and another 4,000 were kept busy in his lumber camps. Algonquin Park had just been created when Booth's railway was constructed through it southern portions, and its presence was the influencing factor in the park's development. Summer camps, elegant resorts and hotels were built, and lumbering operations and towns opened up.

The railway had its eastern terminus in Ottawa, and it worked west to Arnprior, through Renfrew, along the south shore of Golden Lake to Killaloe, where it continued on past Wilno and into Barry's Bay, the divisional point. Here it

skirted around Carson Lake, then picked up the course of the Opeongo River and came into Madawaska. Through the rocky terrain the railway continued on to Whitney and into Algonquin Park with stations at Canoe Lake, Joe Lake and Cache Lake. It then cut through to Scotia Junction about fourteen miles north of Huntsville and continued westerly, through to Parry Sound with a station at Rose Point, and its western terminus at Depot Harbour.

The arrival of the railway acted like a transfusion to Barry's Bay. Now it was more than just a lumber town; it was a railway divisional point complete with a roundhouse, a fine station and water tower (the latter two are still standing). If the town had been planning a monument instead of a water tower, a more impressive approach to the structure would have been difficult to find. A dramatic pattern is created by the division of the tracks as they fan out to the east and the west, making an excellent frame for the weather-worn, red, wooden water tower.

Thomas Murray's recollections of the first train in Barry's Bay, and the days of the railway's construction, have the feeling of pioneer times about them. Almost every farmer he knew, or anyone owning a horse, became a railway employee because of the steady pay. As a boy he was small for his age and "crazy about railroading," even though he nearly killed himself with overwork as a railway employee. Eventually he had to give it up for easier work in the sawmill.

Barry's Bay's first station agent was a pugilist, John Mulloy, who always kept his boxing gloves at work so that he would be ready to spar with anyone who shared his enjoyment of the sport. For several summers the station was treated to a taste of opulence and glamour when the private train belonging to the Governor of Massachusetts was parked on a siding, while he holidayed in the area. Knots of people gathered constantly to marvel at this elegant train, which had thirteen complete bathrooms!

John Oyle, first train conductor on the Ottawa, Arnprior & Parry Sound Railway, was regarded with esteem by everyone, and other men passing him on the street would doff their hats with respect. No conductor was ever more proud of his job, or uniform. Sunday was the day he savoured the full importance of his position through his dramatic appearance in church. Wearing his well-pressed uniform, he arrived at church just as the congregation had seated itself, then he strode with dignity down the full length of the aisle to the first pew, where he settled himself down. As Thomas Murray remarked, "There was a glory to being a conductor in those days."

When J. R. Booth built his railway, his prime reason was to provide rapid transportation for lumber. The railway did that, certainly, but it provided other services as well. Everyone who lived along the line benefited in many ways, and for the young Murray, and other young people, the railway meant an opportunity to visit the Canadian National Exhibition in Toronto. The special coaches on the train provided them with a real taste of high living. Mr. Murray remembers that "we had lunch at Eaton's store in Toronto, spent the rest of the day at the fair . . . bought cream soda pop from the newsboy on the train . . . and had something to talk about all winter." Mr. Murray made many trips to Toronto on that same train in later years, when he became a member of the provincial government's cabinet during the time Mitchell Hepburn was Ontario's premier.

Tom Murray was on the first train in to Madawaska. It was just a work train, and he rode sitting on a box nailed to the floor of a flatcar. In the village today, only the shell of the great railway centre of the Ottawa, Arnprior & Parry Sound Railway is visible. Exploring the ruins is a startling experience. Thirty-five trains a day used to thunder down this line, and in the Madawaska roundhouse and yards, there were always at least twenty-five steam locomotives. Now it is silent, completely abandoned. The roofs are gone from every building, though the high, stone walls remain. Walls of the pits have crumbled, and are now filled with weeds and broken masonry. Through crevices in the cement, lilac bushes have taken root and seem to be thriving on debris left over from an old railway. A single

< *Barry's Bay Station*

Ruins of Madawaska roundhouse

railway track caked with rust skirts the edges of this once-busy complex and is almost obliterated by the tall grass. Down the line, a small, asphalt-shingled shed displays the name "Madawaska" on its board.

Many of Ontario's independent railways failed during their construction, or shortly after, but J. R. Booth's 264-mile-long Ottawa, Arnprior & Parry Sound Railway reached its goal, and prospered. On August 11, 1899, it was consolidated with the Canadian Atlantic Railway, and in 1905, both became amalgamated with the Grand Trunk. Although J. R. Booth's railway exists only in history today, he would never have thought of its departure as a failure. It successfully met the need of the time, and when the job was complete, there was no further need for its existence. Privately-owned railways, and the great "lumber kings" of the last century all contributed richly to Ontario's unique railway history.

KINGSTON

It was standing room only on special trains when hordes of jubilant people streamed into Kingston on July 1, 1867. The banners read "Home Town Boy Makes Good!" "Confederation of Canada." There was a twenty-one gun salute from the militia, bands blaring patriotic airs leading parades, fireworks exploding even before daybreak, church bells — Kingston had never seen such a celebration, nor was it likely to again.

Twenty-four years later on Wednesday, June 10, 1891, another special train came to town, but there were no shouts of joy that day. Sir John A. Macdonald, who for all but six years of his lifetime had thought of Kingston as "home," the man who had brought confederation to Canada and who had become Canada's first prime minister, was being brought home for the last time, to be buried beside his mother in the cemetery in Cataraqui.

The flags which had flown so victoriously in Kingston on that memorable day in 1867 were now lowered to half-mast, and the mournful tolling of church bells could be heard when the slow-moving train came to a halt in front of Kingston City Hall, at the Kingston & Pembroke Railway. Cadets from Kingston's Royal Military College formed a guard of honour around the casket.

Sir John had always been a connoisseur of fine architecture, and it's certain he would have approved of being brought to this elegant station on his final journey to Kingston. The handsome, limestone station that had been built in 1885 by the popular and imaginative architect William Newlands, had six gabled dormers gracing its bellcast roof, and spectacularly beautiful, stained-glass fanlights.

The Kingston & Pembroke Railway had been chartered in 1871, but was not completed until June 1875. Actually, it never was completed as originally planned; upon reaching Renfrew (a distance of 103.6 miles) an agreement was made with the Canada Central Railway to use its line into Pembroke rather than building another one.

Mining and lumbering were the big interests in northern and central Ontario at this time, and railway promoters Benja-

min Folger and Charles Gildersleeve of Kingston were confident that the Kingston & Pembroke would bring tremendous revenue to town. The project did enjoy some success, but when the lumbering business began to wane and passenger business dropped, the railway was absorbed by the Canadian Pacific Railway in 1913.

The tradition among railway employees of coining nicknames for the railways began right at the beginning with the Ontario, Simcoe and Huron Union Railway (nicknamed the Oats, Straw and Hay Railway). Every newly-built railway knew that its employees would soon coin a nickname for it, and some of the nicknames could be highly unflattering. Kingston & Pembroke Railway employees weren't too unkind, they called the line the old "Kick and Push."

If a passenger had a long wait for his train in the K.&P. station, his time could be agreeably spent at any window watching the constant activity all around. In the harbour, tall-masted ships were being loaded from incoming trains, and the outward-bound ship traffic provided many a glorious picture for the viewer when lake breezes caught their great sails. And across from the station was the bustling activity of the great

1912 newspaper picture of Kingston's water front

Present-day CN Turbos meet at Kingston ▷

Kingston Hall, built in 1843. Behind the City Hall was Kingston's famous market square where each week farmers and buyers came to town on the Kingston & Pembroke Railway. From the station, stalls could be seen, their counters piled high with great baskets of fruits and vegetables.

To the east of the railway station was the handsome red-brick firehall (now a restaurant). It was built in 1887 by another well-known architect of the time, John Power. Railway passengers must surely have hoped that fire would break out somewhere in Kingston while their train sat at the station, because of the rare action they would witness. Firemen were alerted by the blowing of a bugle. Then the crews of the three, two-wheeler, horse-drawn rigs raced along each side of the fire-fighting equipment. (To be a fast sprinter was indeed an asset to a fireman in those days, because the only firemen to receive pay were the men of the first crew to arrive at the scene of the fire.) The fire chief made a dramatic arrival by cantering up in his private buggy.

Train passengers must have looked forward to their visits to a railway station surrounded by so much of interest, built with such superb quality and style, and where there was the promise of almost constantly changing action. The old "Kick and Push" station is now owned by the Kingston Chamber of Commerce, and it's still a delightful place to visit. The tracks and train shed are gone, but out in front stands one of CPR's retired steam engines, a 10-wheeler called #1095, built in Kingston, and now serving as a memorial to Sir John A. Macdonald, whose determination brought about the first transcontinental railway in Canada, the CPR.

Surrounding the K.&P. station is Confederation Park, built in the Centennial Year. Beautiful gardens and paths, and a fountain spanned by a 70-foot arch, provide delightful surroundings in which to sit and contemplate the history of Kingston, whose original character appears to have improved with age. The restoration and preservation of its historic buildings has been important to the heritage-conscious residents of this city.

Passengers arriving in Kingston on the Grand Trunk Railway, which was completed in this area in 1856, came in at the old station still standing at the end of Montreal Street. There was dignity and importance in the very name of the Grand Trunk Railway, because it was Canada's first truly great railway.

The influence of its British engineers, Peto, Brassey and Betts, who had years of experience in British and European railway building, was apparent in this Canadian line. Although Canada was over twenty years behind England and the United States in railway building, when the Grand Trunk engineers completed their line between Montreal and Sarnia in 1859, they had succeeded in creating the longest railway in the entire world.

Up until 1860, all their railway stations had great similarity of design and, with the exception of Brighton, were constructed from limestone. The smaller stations had five bay windows, and the larger ones usually had seven. Each station had four chimneys, one at each corner of the roof. These early limestone stations were solid and permanent. However, when the Grand Trunk began to experience financial problems in the 1860s, new railway stations along the line were built out of cheaper materials such as lumber or brick.

Many examples of the standardization of design in GTR stations built in the 1850s can still be seen at Prescott, Napanee, Ernestown, Port Hope, Bowmanville, Georgetown and St. Marys. The larger stations had a common waiting room and a separate area for the ladies. There was always a ticket office, a telegraph office, baggage room and storage room.

The two largest, limestone railway stations built by the GTR can still be seen today: one at Kingston Junction, and the other in Belleville. However, only the latter still serves as a passenger station. Both are two-story in height and have Mansard roofs with gabled dormers.

When the Grand Trunk Railway began its plans for Kingston, a considerable piece of property east of the city was purchased, and a collection of buildings went up in piecemeal order. This area was eventually to be known as the Kingston Station Village. Dorothea Druce of Kingston, who was born

Kingston & Pembroke Railway Station

1912 GTR poster at Kingston Station

GRAND TRUNK RAILWAY SYSTEM

The Double Track Route

To MONTREAL, with direct service to Quebec, Sherbrooke and Portland, also direct connections to Boston, Springfield, New England Points, New York and all Points South, St. John, N.B., Halifax and Points in Maritime Provinces. To TORONTO, HAMILTON, NIAGARA FALLS, BUFFALO, LONDON, DETROIT and CHICAGO, with direct connections at Chicago for all Points in Western States, California, Pacific Coast and Western Canada.

Four Fast Trains Westbound Daily.

Leaving MONTREAL	9.00 A.M.	9.40 A.M.	7.30 P.M.	10.30 P.M.
KINGSTON	12.25 P.M.	3.04 P.M.	12.20 A.M.	2.48 A.M.
Arriving TORONTO	4.30 P.M.	9.10 P.M.	6.00 A.M.	7.30 P.M.

Four Fast Trains Eastbound Daily:

Leaving TORONTO	7.15 A.M.	9.00 A.M.	8.30 P.M.	8.55 P.M.
KINGSTON	12.35 P.M.	1.08 P.M.	1.40 A.M.	2.46 A.M.
Arriving MONTREAL	7.25 P.M.	6.00 P.M.	7.01 A.M.	7.40 A.M.

THE RAILWAY GREYHOUND OF CANADA.

The "INTERNATIONAL LIMITED," leaving MONTREAL, every day in the year for Toronto and the West, is the "crack" train of Canada and the fastest in the Dominion, 7 1-2 HOURS, MONTREAL TO TORONTO.

Grand Trunk Features.

Velvet-running Roadbed—Excellent Train Equipment—Unexcelled Dining Car Service—Courteous Attention—Modern and Handsome Parlor and Library Cars on Day Trains—Pullman Sleeping Cars of the latest designs on night trains.

J. P. HANLEY, City Passenger and Ticket Agent, Kingston, Ont. 'Phone 99

there, believes she is the last living inhabitant of that village.

Miss Druce's grand-uncle, John Donald, had come to Canada from Scotland in 1851 as a surveyor for the G.T.R. but illness eventually forced him to retire. He then bought the historic Royal Oak Hotel which had been an inn during the stagecoach days on the line between York and Montreal.

Miss Druce's grandparents, William and Sarah Fairbairn, also came from Scotland, where William had been the principal of a boys' school. He was incensed that he could not hold a teaching position in Canada without first taking examinations, and so he became a station agent at the Kingston G.T.R. station. However, a physical disability made the arduous work of having to walk the full length of the railway yards, filling and keeping alight the switch lamps, too great a strain on his health, and he was given the position of a switch operator at the junction of the Kingston & Pembroke Railway and Grand Trunk lines. He bought a home for his family near the switch in the railway village, strangely named "Stoney Lonesome." After some time, his past reputation as a brilliant teacher in Scotland spread, and he was rewarded by the companionship of many of Queen's professors, who frequently walked to the station in the evening for a few hours of good conversation with William Fairbairn. One of his most inspiring visitors was Dr. George Munro Grant, principal of Queen's, whose leadership was largely responsible for the importance of the university today.

A separate building in the Kingston Grand Trunk Village was the station restaurant-saloon. The family who ran the restaurant lived in a splendid apartment on the second floor of the railway station, and through their kindness and skill, Dorothea Druce's mother learned to cook. The chef was pleased with his pupil when she eventually succeeded in baking fifteen pies each day before breakfast.

When the Grand Trunk Railway Company of Canada held its first shareholders' meeting on July 27, 1854, one of the subjects of interest on the agenda was the construction of the Kingston area. It reveals the tremendous changes which have

Kingston Grand Trunk Station, 1856

occurred in construction methods since the 1850s. "Upon the middle division at Kingston, where such works only are being proceeded as requires most time to complete, 650 men and 50 horses are employed. The completion of this division of the line being deferred to one year later than the sections at either end, no larger force than that now employed is necessary."

In the appendix of the G.T.R. 1854 annual report, it notes there are "7,600 men and 1,260 horses employed between Montreal and Toronto." In the same central division there were, at that time, "35 carpenters, 18 sawyers, 24 blacksmiths, 82 masons and stonecutters, 490 labourers." The auditors' report recorded that construction costs for the section of railway between Montreal and Kingston, up to June 30, 1854, had been (in sterling) 3,040 pounds, 8 shillings, 4 pence.

Evidence of the tremendous changes that have occurred in Kingston since the creation of the old railway lines is dramatically apparent from the overhead railway bridge spanning the CN tracks at Highway #2. From the bridge you look down over the new style in railway stations: poured concrete and glass. The sleek yellow Turbo, CN's fastest passenger train, makes her only stop between Montreal and Toronto here, four times daily. The "Ontarian," the "Lakeshore," the "Bonaventure," the "Rapido" and the "Cavalier" also make their appearances here each day, Kingston being one of many stops along the line for them.

The lovely old Kingston & Pembroke Railway station has a daily "trackless train" which takes sightseers on a tour of historic Kingston, and the once-busy Grand Trunk station on Montreal Street, is a showroom for fine, imported crystal.

Passengers travelling on the "Night Express" between Montreal and Toronto in 1860, marvelled at the realization that the train they boarded in Montreal at 6 P.M. would be in Toronto's Union Station at 10:10 A.M. on the following day!

Today, CN's Turbo trains leave Montreal and Toronto simultaneously at 8 A.M. each day (except Sunday), and four hours and thirty-five minutes later, passengers are detraining at their destinations. It is possible to return home on the same day by taking the Turbo which departs from the two major cities at 4:50 P.M.

One wonders what the impression of the original Grand Trunk Railway engineers—Sir S. Morton Peto, Bart., M.P., Thomas Brassey, and Edward Ladd Betts—would be were they to stand on the bridge and watch the streamlined Turbo trains from east and west meet at Kingston's modern station, on their record-breaking journeys between Montreal and Toronto.

THE BROCKVILLE RAILWAY TUNNEL

Halfway through the last century, when Canadians were clamouring for railways and pessimistic doctors issued warnings that train-travelling through tunnels could produce serious lung ailments, the town of Brockville had its heart set on a railway tunnel that would pass right beneath the centre of town. That wish was granted, and in 1860 the Brockville and Ottawa Railway Company completed Canada's first railway tunnel.

Still standing today are the massive oak doors that mark the southern entrance to this historic tunnel. No other tunnel in Canada required doors that had to be closed between the hours of sunrise and sunset to keep out the cattle straying through the streets of Brockville all day.

When construction of the Brockville and Ottawa Railway was proposed in 1852, Canada was gripped by "railway fever." This 132-mile-long line would open up new potential for lumbering communities situated between Brockville and Pembroke. It would be the solution to their transportation problem. Timber could now be shipped directly to the harbour at Brockville, where it would be taken by rafts down the St. Lawrence River to Montreal.

Construction was begun with tremendous confidence in the future of the railway, and the sum of almost two million dollars was pledged to the Municipal Loan Fund by the counties and towns. When surveying parties reached the northern outskirts of town, they suggested two alternative approaches to the harbour. A tunnel could be built beneath the town, or tracks could be taken around the perimeter of the community. The latter would have presented less strain on the finances of the company, but the idea of a tunnel so intrigued the entire town that common sense was pushed aside.

Samuel Keefer, supervising engineer, tried to convince railway promoters of the folly of building a tunnel when, for half the cost, tracks could be run around the outskirts of town. But his protests met deaf ears, and on September 16, 1854, construction was formally begun on this expensive novelty.

The laying of the cornerstone for the Brockville tunnel was the most colourful ceremony the town had ever witnessed

Brockville tunnel prior to being boarded up

— it was not even eclipsed by the official opening of the railway. Adiel Sherwood, sheriff of Leeds and Grenville Counties, who as a boy had come to Brockville by batteau with his U.E.L. parents, was given the honour of laying the cornerstone. A parade made up of every organization in town marched through the streets, led by a band. There were the Sons of Temperance, the Knights of Jericho, Freemasons, the Oddfellows, the mayor and town council, directors and engineers of the Brockville and Ottawa Railway, and most of the population of the town. A salvo of fifteen rounds by the local militia brought the celebration to a noisy climax.

Restlessness and disenchantment grew among residents in town when progress on their tunnel came to a halt in 1855. Railway contractors, Sykes, Debergue & Co., ran into financial difficulties, and subcontractors, John Booth and Son, who had already poured $20,000 of their own money into the construction of the tunnel, refused to continue. Disgruntled navvies, who hadn't received wages for several weeks, gave vent to their anger by commandeering and eventually destroying the carriage belonging to a company executive.

Stormy debates raged in Brockville's town council, with

many members favouring the discontinuation of tunnel construction. The final decision was put to the people, who voted unanimously to continue the project. And so, on December 31, 1860, the tunnel was officially opened for traffic.

The track began at the waterfront, in line with Blockhouse Island. It then ran north to the market place where it entered the tunnel, ran beneath Victoria Hall, continued north directly under old Market Street and finally emerged at Pearl Street, 1,712.3 feet from the entrance to the tunnel.

A year before the completion of the Brockville tunnel the railway had initiated passenger service to Perth, forty-six miles north of Brockville. Passengers who crowded into the two, little, wooden coaches for that first trip on January 25, 1859, would not easily forget the day's events. Forty-below-zero weather created constant delays, and nine-and-a-half hours after its departure the train limped into Perth with the coaches fastened to the locomotive with rope, because the couplings had broken apart. One can only imagine the discomfort of passengers in those early days of Canadian railroading: dining cars had not yet been thought of, heating was crude and ineffective and there were no plumbing facilities.

Problems for the Brockville and Ottawa Railway did not cease with the completion of its tunnel, nor at the beginning of rail service. Funds were depleted when the line reached Sand Point, but after an amalgamation with the Canada Central Railway, the rails finally reached Callander. The entire operation was absorbed by the CPR in 1881.

Further colour was added to this historic Brockville and Ottawa Railway when Blockhouse Island in the St. Lawrence River was chosen as the site of the southern terminus. After joining the island to the mainland with fill, workshops and a roundhouse were built. During the cholera epidemic of 1832, victims were isolated on the island. After a ship was sunk in the river during the Rebellion of 1837, a blockhouse was built. However, its ability to protect Brockville against marauders was never put to the test. The local militia fired a few rounds of cannon balls at the solid old fort at the celebration of the rail-

way's opening, but its demolition came about one night when vandals set fire to it.

There isn't a trace of railway buildings on Blockhouse Island today. Gone, too, are the tracks which once led from the waterfront to the portal of the famous tunnel, which saw its last train in 1954. No decision has been made providing a new future for the tunnel, and most residents of Brockville would be incensed if it were demolished. No matter what its fate, this first railway tunnel built in Canada by the Brockville and Ottawa Railway will surely retain its reputation: an engineering feat, or folly—probably it's been a bit of both.

Steam locomotive coming out of the Brockville tunnel

GANANOQUE

Have you ever fished from the open window of a railway coach while your train stopped at a station? Have you ever gone into a railway station and bought a 25¢ return ticket to the local graveyard? And have you ever walked the fulll length of a railway line in less time than required by the train? You have? Then you must have travelled on that little line known as "The T.I." Its real name was the Thousand Island Railway — a six-mile line running from the wharf at Gananoque to the junction of the Grand Trunk Railway (now owned by CNR). From 1889 until 1957, passengers shuttled back and forth on this railway, and old-time employees are as proud of their association with it as if they had been with one of the big, powerful companies that ran straight across the country.

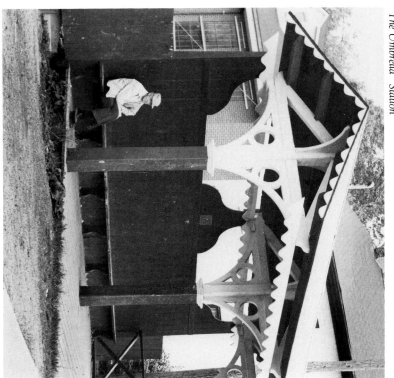

"The Umbrella" Station

Passengers boarding the train at the Junction, to come down into Gananoque, certainly got their money's worth out of the short trip. The line zigzagged all around town, crossing bridges at unexpected places, before arriving at the harbour with its spectacular view.

Trains departing from the frame station on the waterfront proceeded northward along the west bank of the Gananoque River. They then crossed a curved, iron bridge which brought them out to the first station on the line, known as "The Umbrella." Within railway station architecture this building must surely be regarded as an oddity; it's a wooden structure with a roof but no walls. A long bench with a high back could be called the waiting room, and sheltering it is a roof with a most imaginative trim. The whole town would rebel if their beloved "Umbrella" were demolished!

After leaving the Umbrella Station, the train moved on to the cemetery, continued to Cheeseboro, and then it was non-stop to the Gananoque Grand Trunk station. Because of the tremendous areas where the engineer had to travel at almost a snail's pace — street crossings, railway bridges, etc., — it's doubtful that any locomotive ever exceeded ten miles an hour during the entire six-mile trip.

Although the Thousand Island Railway was frequently the butt of jokesters, it did serve a worthwhile purpose. The Rathbun Company, who built it, required transportation for their lumber from the interior forests. Timber was shipped to Gananoque Junction, then switched to the short line, where it was then transferred to ships for overseas markets. The Rathbun Company of Deseronto, one of the most powerful lumber companies in Canada, built the Thousand Island Railways as well as two other small lines: the Bay of Quinte Railway and the Oshawa Railway.

In Gananoque they built a single-track Swing Bridge at the mouth of the Gananoque River, along Water Steet, to accommodate the Byers and Penn Manufacturers of Carriage, Car and Locomotive Springs. The bridge was always a popular spot for youngsters who were intrigued by the bridge's method of opera-

tion. It required several men to manoeuvre the rotating machinery with a series of long poles.

The powerful locomotives needed on large railroads were unnecessary along the Thousand Island line, and the locomotives used by the company were small and odd in appearance. The last one to provide passenger service was retired in 1962, and it now sits on display just to the east of the old railway station, which is presently used as a restaurant. For some reason this locomotive was always called "Susan Push."

"Susan Push" had a busy schedule to keep at the Junction, meeting all the passenger trains from Toronto and Montreal. Passengers spending time at the Junction station during the summer months must have found it pleasant because of the exquisite gardens which surrounded the building. Before the days of automobiles, families would frequently pack up a lunch, hitch the horse to the democrat, and drive out to the Junction for a Sunday outing.

Ross Lloyd, who began working as an expressman with the Thousand Island Railway in 1918, still lives in Gananoque and enjoys recalling early experiences on this old line. It had been his life-long ambition to be an engineer, but he had to first serve time in the express office, then wiping engines, and then as a fireman. After several years he finally became an engineer, and retired in this capacity in 1961. Even on this small line, working hours were long. Mr. Lloyd's day shift began at 6 A.M. and ended at 4 P.M. And if he were on the night shift, he worked from 4 P.M. until 4 A.M.

The elegance of the old wooden coaches on the T.I.R. always impressed Mr. Lloyd. He liked the rich, pine-green paint and the ornamental gold lettering along the sides of the coaches. Upholstery in the coaches had originally been a turkey red, but years of exposure to coal smoke gradually seasoned its colour.

Like every good railway, the T.I.R. had its caboose, but it eventually had to be converted into a snowplow. When one of the double-ended T.I.R. locomotives jumped the track in a snowstorm, even that was insufficient, and additional plows

and the "hook" had to be called in from the Grand Trunk Railway.

Among retired railwaymen, especially those of the steam era, there is a closely-knit camaraderie, and Ross Lloyd still has his closest friends among old-time railwaymen. Many employees who joined the Thousand Island Railway in 1918 with Mr. Lloyd still live in Gananoque.

During the years of prohibition in Canada, all ports of entry along the St. Lawrence had to be alerted to the imaginative deceptions conceived by smugglers. The story of the farmer who successfully tricked customs officers at the Ivy Lea Bridge (just east of Gananoque), has become legendary. His heavy farm waggon, pulled by two typical farm horses, crossed over into Canada almost daily with a load of manure. The farmer's routine never changed. He would return home later in the day with an empty waggon. The driver was a rather bland-appearing man, and he and his goods didn't arouse any suspicion until one day the Canadian Customs Officers were tipped off that this was a load of liquor being carried in, right under their very noses. They thought it was an enormous joke and could scarcely wait for the farmer's arrival that day. Right on schedule the waggon pulled up, piled high with a particularly fresh load of sheep manure. When asked by the officers what he was carrying, the farmer gave his usual answer and he was then instructed to unload the waggon right where it stood. The officers accused him of being a smuggler. With an expression of deep offence, the farmer said that if he was being mistrusted they were welcome to unload his waggon, but he would have no part in it himself. Motorists, growing impatient to cross the bridge, sided with this innocent-looking man and prodded the officers to do the unloading themselves. Not a case or bottle was found! Thoroughly humiliated by now, the officers ordered the "farmer" to load up his waggon and get on his way. Once again he refused. They had unloaded it, he said, and they could now reload it. It would appear that the "farmer" had also been tipped off that day! Until the end of Prohibition he continued his profitable fertilizer business, always using the same port of

Last locomotive used on the Thousand Island Railway

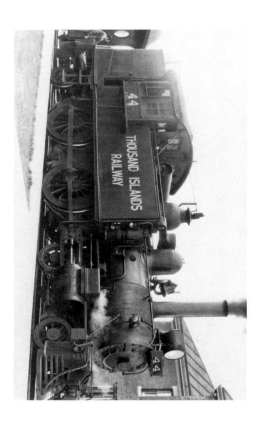

entry, and was never again challenged by the authorities. Motorists in Gananoque still slow down at all the railway crossings, but they are not apt to see any traffic on the rusting tracks. The old frame station at the wharf is still a busy place though, feeding passengers waiting for excursion boats, and accommodating photographers who delight in photographing the last locomotive used for passenger service on the Thousand Island Railway — #500.

It surprises most visitors to learn that a six-mile-long railway could have been profitable. And few people are aware that short railways in Ontario were not really uncommon in the last century. There were at least a dozen under 30 miles in length. The Galt and Guelph Railway, built in 1855, was only 4 miles long. The Peterborough and Chemong Lake, built in 1859, was 12 miles long. There was the line from Schomberg to Aurora of 14 miles; the Guelph Junction, 16.2 miles and the Tillsonburg, Lake Erie and Pacific, built in 1896, was short only 2,884 miles of its 3,000-mile goal to the Pacific. The shortest line in all of Canada (if not in the entire world) was exactly 1⅛ miles from end to end. It was called the Huntsville & Lake of Bays Railway, or the Portage Railway. Its only train was known as the "Portage Flyer!"

Although the Thousand Island Railway didn't hold the record for being the shortest railway, it did establish a reputation of kinds for itself. Where else could a railway passenger sit in the comfort of a red velour, railway-coach seat and fish in the St. Lawrence River?

WATCHMAN'S TOWERS

Builders of early Grand Trunk Railway watchman's towers would be dumbfounded today by the sight of the CN Tower overshadowing their few remaining structures in Toronto's rail yards. All the facts and figures surrounding this tower, which is the tallest free-standing tower in the world, would have sounded like sheer fantasy one hundred years ago.

Before the days of overpasses and underpasses, it was customary in most cities for railways to protect pedestrians from approaching trains by long, wooden gates which were raised and lowered by a watchman. A cabin, built on stilts about thirty feet high, gave the watchman a perfect bird's-eye view down the tracks. A brass train bell suspended from the front of the cabin was pulled by a rope to warn pedestrians of danger, and a heavy, iron lever manipulated the gates. The old cabins, scarce as they are today, remain almost unchanged except for the addition of an electric buzzer which announces the approach of a train.

These ancient, wooden cabins have become an oddity and must surely be startling for the uninitiated, seeing them for the first time. Toronto, with all its tracks, required many of these cabins before the days of automation. Now, only two remain: one at the Strachan Avenue crossing, just east of the Canadian National Exhibition, and the other at the Junction in the city's west end.

Jobs in the cabins were usually held by partially physically-disabled employees, who were unable to cope with heavy work. Frequently, railwaymen who had lost an arm or leg in a train wreck were given the job.

Joe Cadieux takes the day shift at the Strachan Avenue tower. An hour there is similar to continuous exposure to an orchestra's percussion section. The old cabin barely settles down before the next train highballs through. A warning bell sounds in the cabin, the brass bell clangs outside the window, bells ring and red lights flash at the crossing — and just a few feet below you, the freight train thundering down the track seems determined to shake the old wooden cabin right off its spindly legs. Joe's "green thumb" is apparent in the profusion of petunias growing in flower boxes outside the windows. Even the small patch of ground at the foot of the steps has been put to use. Two healthy rows of cabbages seem to have thrived on soil which appears to be mainly cinders.

Joe's job must surely have been the most sought-after among watchmen, during the construction of the CN Tower. A completely unobstructed view gave him the opportunity to follow the tower's progress right up to the moment helicopter Olga soloed in for the topping-off ceremony.

Anacletho Cappadocia, another watchman with many years of railway service, is at the Junction tower. His enthusiasm for railways is as great today as it was during his childhood in Italy. He still recalls the excitement of riding on a train to Rome with his father. From his tower on the main lines of CP and CN, the sleek "Canadian" and "Supercontinental" can be seen picking up passengers at their West Toronto stations, just a few yards apart. This is also the end of the line for cattle heading for the stockyards. A more cheerful train to view is a steam excursion pulled by CN's 6060. When it passes through, the Junction is filled with photographers and train buffs, all out to see the last of the great steam engines.

A traffic tie-up at the John Street crossing in Toronto several years ago, which almost brought about law suits against the railways, has become legendary. On a sweltering summer day the watchman (known for his reliance on the bottle) decided to refresh himself at a nearby beverage room. His intention to be absent just long enough to have one drink must have disappeared at some point, and the time stretched into almost two hours. During this time the crossing was blocked by the gates that the watchman had decided should be lowered. By the time his superintendent was located and a key found to unlock the cabin door, a traffic jam to end all traffic jams had built up. The railway decided it could manage without the unfortunate man's services, and a ruling was promptly brought in to control the length of time traffic could be detained by lowered gates.

Among railwaymen, probably the best-known tower in Toronto is Cabin D, built by the Grand Trunk about 100 years

*Joe Cadieux, tower watchman
at Strachan Avenue, Toronto*

Herb Stitt at John Street tower, Toronto

John Street tower with legs removed. Tower is now gone. ⟩

ago. It's a narrow, two-storey building squeezed among a maze of tracks at the west end of the Toronto yards. It was here that train traffic used to be controlled. A bank of hand-operated levers adjusted the semaphores that told the engineers which track they would be taking.

Watchman's towers — water towers — coal silos — all became obsolete in the 1950s when steam locomotives were replaced by diesel engines. Their very names will soon have passed. It's certain that early railroad builders never visualized railroads of the future, operating without these once-so-necessary structures.

When you're out for a Sunday drive in the country you frequently cross a pair of rusting railway tracks, and there's something mysterious about them just appearing there. Where are they going? Standing nearby is the familiar white and black railway-crossing sign, but it doesn't provide any additional information. Most of these forgotten lines were built at least one hundred years ago, by railway companies whose names are unfamiliar to us today because they are now all a part of either the CPR or the CNR. It could have been the Midland Railway that built those tracks you just drove over, or the Credit Valley Railway, the Cobourg & Peterborough, the Wellington, Grey & Bruce, or perhaps the Brockville, Westport & Sault Ste. Marie Railway.

If you sat all day at some of these crossings you might not see a single train, and certainly not a passenger train. The majority of the old lines are now branch lines, and at infrequent intervals, a way-freight train bowls down the track hauling a few, ancient boxcars, and everyone's favourite, the caboose. Up until 1970, most of these lines still had modified passenger service joining rural communities with main lines of the railways but, one by one, they were discontinued.

"Mixed trains" travelled along every rural line and were regarded by passengers with a somewhat patronizing air. The same crew members always seemed to be on the "mixed," and they knew the passengers by their first names. They knew their habits and never considered it an imposition to relay messages for passengers to someone in the next town. Train crews on these country lines adhered to the company's safety rules, but adjusted other regulations to fit the occasion. When a passenger who travelled frequently between Palmerston and Southampton complained about the discomfort of the coach seats, a comfortable overstuffed chair and footstool were put in the baggage compartment, and there she rode in deluxe style for many years.

On another branch line, where the daughter of the track foreman was a botanist with a keen interest in butterflies, the train conductor permitted her to ride in the baggage car. There,

CN *way-freight at Palmerston*

she could swing out her butterfly net at every prize specimen she saw along the way.

On the 16-mile Listowel to Linwood CPR branch line, which connected with the Goderich subdivision, engineer Joe Fair ran old #7048 (built in 1882) from the day the line opened in 1908 until it closed in the 1950s. When the last scheduled train ran out of Listowel that day, Joe Fair was asked to take the throttle, even though he had been retired for several years. Number 7048 was Joe's engine, and no one ever dared dispute it. J. W. Leonard, General Manager of CP at that time, was Joe's brother-in-law, and he ensured that any parts or tools Joe needed to keep his engine in good running order were sent along promptly. They said Joe's one-pit engine house was

Old coal chute

as well stocked with tools and equipment as any large, modern roundhouse. Incidentally, the CPR paid honour to their General Manager, Mr. Leonard, by giving his name to a point on one of their lines. However, they reversed the spelling and called it "Dranoel."

Joe Fair spent every Sunday in the engine house cleaning and tuning up his beloved engine, and Herb Stitt, who was Joe's fireman for two years, said it was his job to shine the brass and copper. He "kept the brass and copper in the cab shined up like a jewellery shop, as well as the bell and number plate." From this little 16-mile branch line, the CPR used to get $75,000 in business annually. But it's gone now; the tracks are lifted, and the station used as a hydro substation.

Way-freight trains which rattle over these neglected lines are the final connection with robust, old-time railroading, and as for travelling in them — their swaying, rolling and jolting is an experience only for seasoned railwaymen! A string of dusty boxcars and a couple of greasy tank cars usually make up these trains — rolling stock all too disreputable in appearance for the main lines. Six days a week they hurtle around rural Ontario picking up carloads of furniture from well-known factories in Hanover, Kincardine or Durham, as well as loads of grain and cattle and other commodities.

One of CPR's best-known Ontario branch lines runs out of Orangeville, and is known as the Orangeville subdivision. In the middle of the night, a way-freight called the "Moonlight" starts out from Streetsville, heading north for Orangeville. It passes through Meadowvale, Brampton, Snelgrove, Cheltenham, Inglewood, Forks of the Credit, Cataract (where it meets up with the Elora subdivision of the CPR), then continues on to Alton, and finally comes into Orangeville, a total of 34.6 miles. Here it picks up any cars bound for Toronto, then heads back to Streetsville, arriving there before daylight.

During the 1880s, Orangeville was a divisional point on the Toronto, Grey and Bruce Railway, and judging by the number of tracks around the station grounds it's obvious that Orangeville was a very busy spot. However, only the way-

freight uses the line now, and the coal chute, roundhouse, turntable, water tower, and the once-popular station restaurant all have vanished. Despite its peeling paint, the handsome, old station is still pleasant to see with its circular waiting room, conical roof, and colourful gardens tended by the local horticultural society.

What the Orangeville yard lacks in size and activity, it makes up for in noise — but few complaints are ever registered. The majority of Orangeville residents rather enjoy having this link with the railway. Action at the station begins any time after 7:30 each morning with the sounds of protesting boxcars lunging down the line, as they are made up into their proper

Rural railway bridge

(from l. to r.)
Herbert Stitt (retired CPR engineer),
Fred Worthington (trainman)
and Peter Hawke (conductor)

order. When the caboose is finally coupled on at the end of the line of cars, the brakeman waves a lantern from the tail end, the crossing bell at the roadway starts ringing, the engineer gives a few lusty toots on the whistle, and suddenly the string of cars is lurching down the line that twists and winds its way through residential back yards in the south part of town. After crossing Highway #9, the train enters Dufferin County's farmland where, daily, the same herds of cattle flee in panic at the sight of this familiar train.

Herbert Stitt, 80-year-old retired CPR engineer from Toronto, who was engineer on the Orangeville way-freight for many years, recently accompanied the way-freight train crew on a nostalgia-filled trip to Owen Sound. Jack Brawley and several other old-time railwaymen of Mr. Stitt's era were at the station to greet him and give him a send-off. Both conductor Peter Hawke, and trainman Fred Worthington, members of the crew that day, had worked with Mr. Stitt years ago.

Their entire trip to Owen Sound was filled with reminiscences, and their descriptions of the winter of '47 made one hope that winter would withhold its fury until one returned home that day! Blizzards blew for weeks on end in that memorable winter, and on one occasion it took seventy-three hours to reach Owen Sound. As fast as the snowplow cut through a gap, blowing winds filled it up again. Herb Stitt pulled out snapshots from his wallet which showed seven steam locomotives pushing a snowplow through this same area in that particular winter.

There were a lot of happy memories on that trip for Herb Stitt, especially when the train passed familiar farms where the same people he had known long ago were still there, waving to the train crews from their farmhouse windows. He recalled, with mouth-watering detail, the hearty meals train crews used to enjoy in the caboose. Thick stews bubbled all day in heavy, iron pots on the wood-stove, and slabs of hot apple pie, washed down with black coffee, boosted the morale of tired railwaymen whose work never seemed to be done in winter storms.

It was dusk when the way-freight pulled in to Orangeville, and a steady fall of light snow was not a welcome sight to the train crew. There seemed to be ominous overtones to the three, bright red, freshly-painted snowplows waiting on the passing tracks. They gave the impression that they were aware of things to come. Herb Stitt reminded the crew that it was in Orangeville in 1883 that the first rotary snowplow was successfully built and put into service by the Leslie Brothers.

For CPR way-freight train #72, work was finished for the day, and no other trains would use that line until tomorrow. In many parts of Ontario, in fact all across Canada, rural communities have their own "Orangeville" railway stories, and leading into these small towns, along the rusting rails, is a wealth of history which probably will never be recorded.

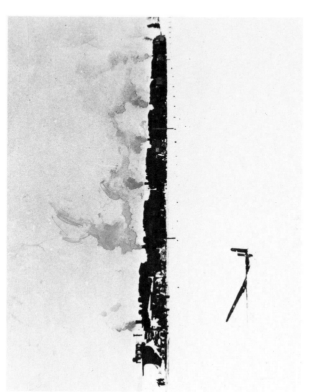

Winter of 1944, seven locomotives pushing snowplow to open CPR Teeswater branch line

Faces from the Steam Era

From the moment the first engineer climbed into a locomotive cab, train engineers became heroes in the eyes of almost everyone. Songs were dedicated to their adventures, and poets were inspired by their fearlessness. The engineer ruled in the hearts of the people and in his cab, but in the train, the boss was the conductor.

It was easy to identify the conductor because of the impressive array of gold service stripes on his uniform sleeve. His voice boomed through the coach when he swung open the vestibule door and shouted, "Have your tickets ready, please!" Sometimes he was grouchy, possibly because his feet ached from the miles they covered as he walked from one end of the train to the other.

Spending a night on the "sleeper" provided the traveller with conversational food for months. And it is unlikely that he quickly forgot the quiet efficiency of the porter who made up his berth, or the comfort the man's presence provided in the muffled darkness of the sleeping car.

The "flyer" and the "express" trains would be met at the big depots by an oil-smeared trainman, carrying a hammer. His job was to tap the coach wheels with his hammer, while listening for defects.

All trainmen, including the brake man and fireman, had to be of hardy stock since they led rough and sometimes dangerous lives. The trainman experienced little of the railroading glamour that accompanied the jobs of the engineer, conductor or station agent.

The station agent was greatly admired by most young lads. His uniform consisted of his green celluloid eyeshade and black sateen shirt-cuff protectors. He was privy to most of the town gossip and all the news that came in over the wires, but he kept it to himself. Discretion was an important part of a station agent's code of ethics. He worked seven days a week, took pride in his job and would not have traded it with anyone.

Crew of the "Nip and Tuck" train, circa 1900

Lakefield station agent and town doctor, circa 1898

Firemen on early steam locomotives were known as "The Tallow Pots," as it was sheep tallow they used to lubricate the engines.

<Last of the Northerns 4-8-4

Oliver "Happy" Ingle holding train orders on hoop for engineer.

Oliver "Happy" Ingle, last station agent at Petersburg Station. He worked at this CN station for over 25 years. The station was built in 1856, and is standing now at the Doon Pioneer Village near Kitchener.

92

Mr. T.B. Williams, last station agent at Seaforth CNR Station. Station demolished around 1973.

The Hogger (CPR engineer)

Clifford Scott, CPR conductor,
Owen Sound

The conductor was usually known as "The Connie." He has always been in charge of the train. An early railway rule stated that "Conductors must wear shoes while on duty, socks not necessary."

Railway Bygones

The flavour of the old railway stations can very very rarely be recaptured today. It was made up of intangibles, such as the welcome warmth of the potbelly stove, the ticking of the Seth Thomas clock, flies buzzing against the dusty window panes, and the mysterious messages in Morse code which were only understood by that man of genius, the station telegraph operator. Every fibre of a rural railway station was impregnated with the pungent aroma of smoke and kerosene, and no amount of ventilation altered the quality of the aroma. These invisible elements were as much a part of the station as were the waiting room benches.

The daily train timetable was recorded on the blackboard, which hung on the platform, near the doorway to the waiting room. Times were checked and rechecked by the drivers of the hotel's horse-drawn omnibuses, which met every train. Just before train time the town's postmaster would arrive in his buggy to pick up the sacks of mail.

An iron water-pump could be found near the station, and at a discreet distance from the station stood the outdoor privy, genteelly concealed by lilac and honeysuckle bushes.

Travellers in the early part of this century would have marvelled at our modern, matched sets of luggage. Theirs ranged from flimsy wicker grips to heavy leather suitcases. They also carried carpet bags, Gladstone bags, satchels and valises. If the family were making an extended trip, they packed their wardrobes inside large, elaborate trunks (collectors' items today), and a sign of affluence was the number of stickers from steamship lines and hotels covering each trunk.

Changes have taken place in every sector of railway life. There used to be water towers in the days of steam locomotives — tall, ungainly-looking coal shutes protruding over the railway tracks, bunkhouses for weary train crews, white-washed cattle pens at rural stations, smoke-stained roundhouses and turntables. Where could you find them today? They exist only in the memories of retired railwaymen, and in faded photographs in the family album.

Men and pushcart outside the Kleinburg station. It was built by the Toronto, Grey and Bruce Railway in 1870.

Unusual waiting room bench in Clinton railway station

MIDLAND RAILWAY OF CANADA.

TIME TABLE,

No. 6.   No. 6.

TAKES EFFECT ON MONDAY, MAY 27th, 1872.

TRAINS MOVING NORTH.

Miles	STATIONS.	No. 1 BEAVERTON MAIL.	No. 3 LAKEFIELD MAIL.	No. 5 BEAVERTON MIX'D	LAKEFIELD MIXED.	No. 7 WAY FREIGHT.	No. 9
66	† Beaverton, Arr.	12.30 P.M					
58	† Woodville,	12.10		8.00 P.M			
54	* Oakwood,	11.53		7.00			
49	* Cambray,	11.41		6.42			
43	† Lindsay,	11.25d / 11.20a		6.20d / 6.00a			
38	* Kelly's,	11.08		5.38			
33	† Omemee,	10.58		5.20			
28	† Franklin,	10.43		4.55d / 4.35a			
26	* Brunswick,	10.38		4.27			
24	† Bethany,	10.33		4.20			
—							
40	† Lakefield,		12.40 P.M		7.00 P.M		
31	† Peterboro',		12.00d / 11.40a		6.20d / 6.00a		
24	† Fraserville,		11.16		5.36		
18	† Millbrook,	10.15d / 10.10a	11.00d / 10.50a	3.50d / 3.30a	5.20d / 5.02a	7.00d / 6.50a	
14	* Summit,	9.58	10.35	3.12	4.45	6.30	
10	† Campbell's,	9.46	10.18	2.50	4.25d / 4.10a	6.10	
9	* Perrytown,	9.43	10.14	2.45	4.05	6.03	
5	* Quay's,	9.35	10.04	2.35	3.55	5.52	
0	† Port Hope, Dep.	9.20 A.M	9.45 A.M	2.15 P.M	3.35 P.M	5.30 A.M	

TRAINS MOVING SOUTH.

Miles	STATIONS.	No. 2 BEAVERTON MAIL	No. 4 LAKEFIELD MAIL	No. 6 BEAVERTON MIX'D	LAKEFIELD MIXED	No. 8 WAY FREIGHT	No. 10 WAY FREIGHT.
0	† Beaverton, Dep.	3.00 P.M					
8	† Woodville,	3.25		7.30a / 7.42d			
12	* Oakwood,	3.37		8.00			
17	* Cambray,	3.49		8.18			
23	† Lindsay,	4.05a / 4.10d		8.40a / 9.00d			
28	* Kelly's,	4.22		9.22			
33	† Omemee,	4.35		9.40			
38	† Franklin,	4.47		10.00			
40	* Brunswick,	4.52		10.08			
42	† Bethany,	4.57		10.15a / 10.33d			
0	† Lakefield,		1.50 P.M		5.20 A.M		
9	† Peterboro',		2.30a / 3.00d		5.55a / 6.10d		
16	† Fraserville,		3.24		6.32		
48	† Millbrook,	5.15a / 5.20d	3.40a / 3.50d	10.55a / 11.15d	6.50a / 7.00d		1.35a / 1.55d
52	* Summit,	5.30	4.04	11.33	7.17		2.15
56	† Campbell's,	5.43	4.22	11.53	7.37		2.35a / 2.50d
57	* Perrytown,	5.46	4.26	11.58	7.42		2.55
61	* Quay's,	5.54	4.36	12.08	7.53		3.06
66	† Port Hope, Arr.	6.10 P.M	4.55 P.M	12.30 P.M	8.15 A.M		3.30 P.M

* Platform Stations, Trains stop on Signal only.   † Telegraph Stations.   ☛ Heavy Faced Figures denote Train Crossings. The figures set opposite the Stations indicate the leaving time of Trains.

All Trains must start promptly on time. Should any Employee not fully understand this Time Table, or Special Rules on the back, it will be his duty to apply to the head of his department for information. Trains run by Port Hope time, which is 20 minutes slower than Grand Trunk time.

DESTROY FORMER TIME CARDS.

H. G. TAYLOR, Supt. of Motive Power and Trains.

J. B. TRAYES, Printer, TIMES Printing Office, Walton Street, Port Hope.

An engine on the Atlantic and St. Lawrence Railway, December 1856

Water tower at Monkland railway station built from limestone

< *Rural freight shed with old-fashioned trunks and waggons*

Potbelly stove from Petersburg
railway station waiting room

Stained glass window at Kingston & Pembroke Station

BYTOWN AND PRESCOTT RAILROAD.

1851.

Toronto yards from Bathurst Street bridge, 1942

Toronto yards from Bathurst
Street bridge, 1975

Meet Me at the Next Station

Meet me at the next station — farmers are there discussing their crops, school children are watching anxiously for the arrival of the next train, in the evening the young couples will be sitting on the platform benches. . . .

That, of course, is the way it was. Now that the lovable, old "mixed train" has vanished, and almost every local line has been deprived of passenger service, railway stations are disappearing at an alarming rate. Some are padlocked for several years, and then fall victim to vandals. Others are sold and moved away, while others are dismantled by the railway wreckers. Ugly scars remain for a short time where a railway station once stood, but soon the rubble is hidden by the growth of colourful wild flowers. Patches of rhubarb planted long ago by a station agent's wife continue to survive; lilac bushes bloom and spread, and spindly hollyhocks refuse to die.

These stations were the pride of their communities when they were built. The townspeople looked at a station as the town's guarantee of progress, prosperity and glamour. Stations symbolized the utmost in glamour in those early years. So, meet me at the next station — perhaps it's not too late.

INGERSOLL. This station was built by the Great Western Railway, circa 1878, and has been a part of the CNR since 1923.

HASTINGS was on the Grand Junction Railway which ran between Belleville and Peterborough, opening on June 30, 1878. It became consolidated with the Midland Railway of Canada in 1882, and was leased to the Grand Trunk in 1884.

BANCROFT was the southern terminus of the Irondale, Bancroft & Ottawa Railway, a 53-mile line running between Howland and Bancroft. The line was opened on April 25, 1898, and was acquired by the Canadian Northern Ontario Railway in 1910.

WOODSTOCK was built on the main Great Western Line which passed through Woodstock in 1853. This line was taken over by the Grand Trunk Railway in 1882, and by the CNR in 1923.

BLYTH CPR Station. The CPR completed this line which ran between Guelph and Goderich in 1907. The town is about 22 miles east of Goderich.

SEAFORTH was on a line built by the Buffalo and Lake Huron Railway. In 1856 the line went from Fort Erie to Paris; on December 22, 1956, the line was extended from Paris to Stratford, and on June 28, 1858 it was extended from Stratford to Goderich. Seaforth is about 33 miles west of Stratford. The line was taken over by the Grand Trunk Railway in 1875.

WINGHAM was built by the London, Huron & Bruce Railway and the station was the northern terminus of the railway. The line went through in 1876, and was taken over by the Great Western in 1876.

RENFREW. The Canada Central Railway built a line from Almonte to Sand Point, 1867, and from Sand Point to Renfrew March 27, 1873. The line was bought by the CPR in 1881, and continued on to Callander in 1882.

NORWOOD. On August 31, 1884 the Ontario & Quebec Railway built a 98-mile line between Perth and Norwood, and the line continued on to West Toronto, an additional 95 miles. It was purchased by the CPR in 1884. The upper portion of the station was living quarters for the station agent and his family.

WELLAND Junction was on the "Loop Line" of the Great Western Railway which went through Glencoe, St. Thomas, Tillsonburg and Welland Junction. It continued on to Fort Erie, and crossed over to Buffalo.

KLEINBURG Station on the original Toronto, Grey and Bruce Railway line. The line was taken over by the Canadian Pacific Railway on Nov. 1, 1883. The station itself was actually in Nashville, and in 1976 it was moved to the village of Kleinburg and restored by the Boy Scouts of the area.

SUTTON. When the Toronto and Nipissing Railway completed its line between Toronto and Coboconk, in Nov. 1872, the line ran through Stouffville. From this point they built an extension to Lake Simcoe in 1877, with Sutton as the northern terminus. This portion of the railway was called the Lake Simcoe Junction Railway. The entire line was acquired by the Midland Railway in 1882, then by the Grand Trunk Railway in 1884, and finally by the CNR in 1923.

INGERSOLL

HASTINGS

BANCROFT >

WOODSTOCK

BLYTH

SEAFORTH

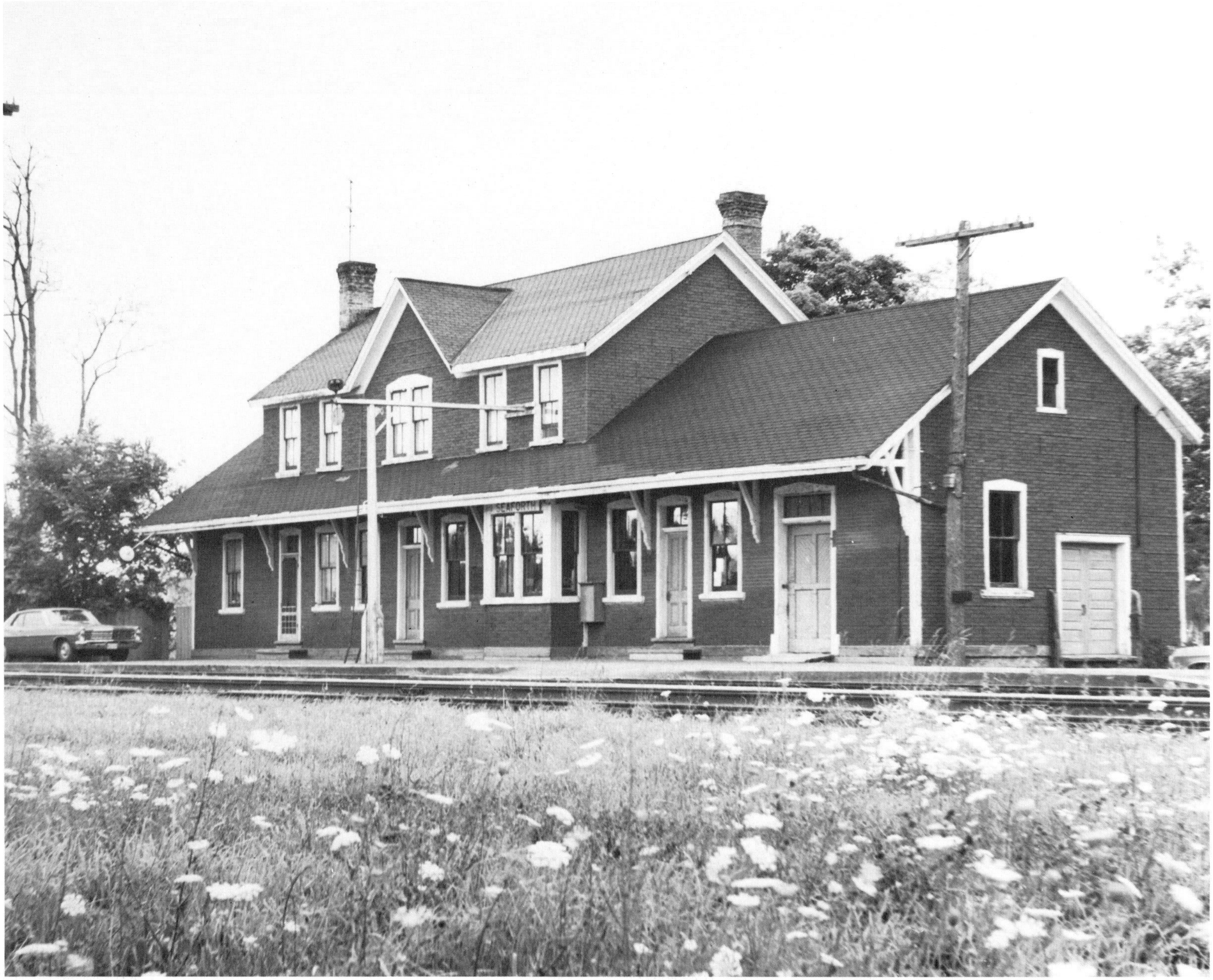

WINGHAM >

WELLAND JUNCTION

KLEINBURG >